"God loves you—three words with such profound meaning. In a society saturated by the world's standard of love, there is no greater time to be reminded of the incredible, personal, and miraculous love of God that will never leave you nor abandon you. Micah Berteau is a gifted leader and pastor who has tailored his personal stories and biblical insight into an encouraging journey for readers to discover God's love that really changes everything."

Brian Houston, Global Senior Pastor of Hillsong Church

"Love changes everything! The love I'm referring to is God's love—a love that is redemptive, relentless, and unconditional. Micah has done an excellent job of unpacking the lessons discovered in the book of Hosea and correlating them to our intrinsic need to love and be loved, and how when you encounter love, you ultimately encounter God—for God is love. I'm excited for the release of *Love Changes Everything* because as each of us becomes rooted in God's extravagant love, we'll experience a freedom and a confidence that empowers us to become who we were created to be. That's the inherent power of love—no one remains the same once true love is experienced!"

John Bevere, bestselling author, minister, and cofounder of Messenger International

"I am amazed at how my son combines humor, content, Scripture, explanations, life pictures, and an incredible Old Testament story in today's vernacular for this book. Watching God direct Micah's steps his entire life, I saw the makings of a man of God. What he has learned, he has walked through. His heart is burdened for this culture that is inundated with division, disunity, and headlines of hate. *Love Changes Everything* hits the reset button. Honestly, it really is an incredible read."

Glen Berteau, senior pastor of The House Modesto and author of *Christianity Lite* and *Christianity to Go*

"In today's culture, affirmation and love are so often found through strangers on social media. With hopes that the right pose or the perfect caption will take away insecurities, people are searching for a shallow love to temporarily fulfill them. In *Love Changes Everything*, Micah Berteau beautifully unpacks the revelation of God's unfailing adoration for us. For as long as I've known Micah, I've admired his heart for people and his passion to share the grace and love of God with every person he meets. This book will leave you with a renewed perspective on how greatly you're loved by the One who is love. No matter your age or season of life, you will be blessed as you read *Love Changes Everything*."

Chris Durso, author of *The Heist: How Grace Robs Us of Our Shame*

"Micah is a living, breathing example of how to live out our one true mission as Christian people: to love. Through his book *Love Changes Everything*, Micah takes you on a journey of biblical reference and lays down the bridge to everyday application that we can then use to go forward and impact the lives of others. Love changes everything around it, but you first have to understand it—the way God intended."

Bryce Petty, former NFL player

"Micah Berteau injects our broken world with the undeniable healing power of love. In *Love Changes Everything*, Micah equips us with the necessary biblically substantiated tools empowering us to explore, embrace, and express the amazing love of God, and with that love . . . change the world!"

Samuel Rodriguez, New Season lead pastor, NHCLC president, author of *You Are Next!*, and executive film producer of *Breakthrough*

LOVE CHANGES EVERYTHING

LOVE

CHANGES
EVERYTHING

FINDING WHAT'S **REAL**

IN A WORLD FULL OF **FAKE**

MICAH BERTEAU

Revell

a division of Baker Publishing Group
Grand Rapids, Michigan

Published by Revell
a division of Baker Publishing Group
PO Box 6287, Grand Rapids, MI 49516-6287
www.revellbooks.com

Printed in the United States of America

Library of Congress Cataloging-in-Publication Data
Names: Berteau, Micah, author.
Title: Love changes everything : finding what's real in a world full of fake / Micah Berteau.
Description: Grand Rapids, MI : Revell, a division of Baker Publishing Group, [2019] | Includes bibliographical references.
Identifiers: LCCN 2019011784 | ISBN 9780800736941 (pbk.)
Subjects: LCSH: God (Christianity)—Love. | Christian life.
Classification: LCC BT140 .B48 2019 | DDC 231/.6—dc23
LC record available at https://lccn.loc.gov/2019011784

19 20 21 22 23 24 25   7 6 5 4 3 2 1

To Lindsey, the best and most beautiful wife ever;
our world-changing boys, Beckham and Braylon;
and any other Berteaus born after this book.
Y'all are my world and I love you more than words!
To my parents for always loving and believing in me.
Love y'all so much!

CONTENTS

Contents

FOREWORD

JENTEZEN FRANKLIN

What an honor it is to be asked to say a few words about Micah Berteau's book, *Love Changes Everything*. If ever we needed a book on love with a powerful word for the age we are in it is now. Micah unpacks the many ways the word "love" is used, abused, and overused by a media and marketing machine famous for exploiting even the most sacred of topics. But rather than focusing solely on the negative ways the world uses this timeless word, he instead provides a much greater context, using the biblical example of Hosea and Gomer to show God's heart and original intent for a truth he created.

We live in a day and age when people are searching for love in all the wrong places and all the wrong faces. Songs are written about it. More movies are made about love than we have time to watch, and television is littered with opportunities to consume the love it sells. Far too often in movies and television love is reduced to physical relationships as millions tune in and accept these shallow versions of love as though they were gospel. But they are not gospel—they are cheap imitations of what God originally intended and desires for us today.

We were made for more. *You* were made for more. It is obvious that our modern culture is obsessed with false notions about love. But you were made to experience far more than a "notion." You were made to experience depths of love designed by the One who created you. Powerful stuff! If human love can change a person, what can the real love of God do? More. So much more. When you try to understand love through human eyes only, it is impossible to see God's plan for your life or for your relationships with close friends and family and those people God places around you on a daily basis. No wonder we aren't seeing God's love and being moved by it like we need to be.

I believe that as you turn each page of *Love Changes Everything*, you will find the Lord speaking directly to you about the very thing that drove him to give his life on the cross—love. I also think that with each new chapter you will add another layer of revelation and will experience love at a whole new level in every relationship. This has been God's plan since the beginning. There's more. Commit to finding out just how much more and invest the time to walk through these chapters. I believe that as you unpack the truths in the pages ahead, you will discover all over again that love truly changes everything.

INTRODUCTION

God proved His love on the Cross. When Christ hung, and bled, and died, it was God saying to the world, "I love you."

Billy Graham

Hey there, friends! Welcome to the beginning of this love expedition. Yes, you are reading a book on the love of Jesus. The powerful, relentless, profound, unshakable, unfathomable, immeasurable, overwhelming, incalculable, incomprehensible, and undeniable love of God. I know what you may be thinking: "What more could I learn that I have not already heard on this topic?" And you are correct that there are some strong books on the love of God. However, when God called me to write this book, I knew there was a message he wanted to release that I could not ignore.

This is more than a book; it is a journey. Everything I write about here has changed my entire perspective on life. I used to be stuck in religion and legalistic living, and then I met real love. God has placed a message on my heart just for you. Seriously, I cannot shake the revelation that has been birthed in my spirit and brought to life through this book. So this is not another typical book on the love of God. It is much more than you may think, and the only way to find out is to keep turning these pages. My prayer is that this book will shift and shape your life forever.

We are all searching for something real. Something tangible that will add value and significance to our lives. Love is vague and vast. Love is well-studied yet highly misunderstood. Love is found down many roads, but it depends on what kind of love you are looking for. People all over the world will do crazy things to find love. But exactly what love are you chasing?

When you know what you're searching for, you can better understand why you do what you do. Is it a love full of feelings? Is it being loved and cherished by someone else that produces a profound sense of validation on your life? Is it temporary pleasure that gives you a sense of authentication, but just for a moment in time? What kind of love do you believe will bring sustaining significance to your being?

The answers to these critical questions will show your ideals and convictions. They will expose the true intentions of your heart. And please, no more "following your heart." Follow the Holy Spirit, not that thing in your chest. This will assist you in finding you. Your security cannot be founded upon a fake reality.

There is fake everywhere we turn. We are offered fake brand-name items. The only reason we spend too much money on a knockoff is to make people think we can afford the real thing. It is a facade. The fake item is not made with the same quality; it will not last but will fall apart. Buying an imitation is more about wanting approval from others so we feel better about ourselves. However, those are fleeting feelings. Here today and gone tomorrow.

Falling in love with fake will always leave you frustrated, especially when it comes to fake love. There are numerous kinds of fake love that will catch your eye and that you can pursue. But there is only one love that can radically and unapologetically tear down the filters of your heart and carry you until your last breath. There is only one love that can take away the urge to settle for anything less than all that you are called to be. There is only one love that can step into the darkest of nights and light up your whole life. There is only one love that violently repels fake. This love—real love—changes everything.

Now let's take a ride that will change your existence. I can't wait to hear how you are impacted by the ensuing words. If you open your heart as you read and let God speak to you, you will never be the same.

THE FIRST MOVE

God loves each of us as if there were only one of us.

Augustine

But *because of his great love for us,* God, who is rich in mercy, made us alive with Christ even when we were dead in transgressions—it is by grace you have been saved.

Ephesians 2:4–5 NIV, emphasis added

I was seven years old. My parents were pastors in Baton Rouge, Louisiana, which is where I was born. However, my dad had just agreed to pastor a church in Modesto, California. This meant we were moving. This was a major life change for a seven-year-old and my first move ever. I was going to lose friends. I was going to lose humidity. I was going to lose crawfish. I was staring right in the face of the biggest change I had ever experienced.

However, I did not know that it would be the journey, not the destination, that would alter my life. Literally, the trip from Louisiana to California shifted everything.

I can remember leaving on a scorching hot Louisiana day. As I climbed into that all-pink 1987 van, I was nervous yet a little excited about this new season. In that van we had a TV with a VCR and Nintendo. I was most excited about that.

We drove into Arlington, Texas, and my parents surprised my two older sisters and me with a trip to Six Flags. Side note: my current church that I planted in 2018 is twenty minutes from this particular theme park. This will prove to be significant, as this fun trip turned into one of the most memorable and impactful moments of my life.

I recall walking into this theme park, filled with so much excitement. I was jumping and screaming with my prepuberty voice, beyond elated at what was about to go down. The moment we walked through the gates I began yelling, "Dad! Dad! I want to ride that ride! Let me ride that ride! Please, please, pleeaassee!" My dad turned and looked at me like I was crazy and said, "Son, that's a hot dog cart." What can I say? It looked like a delicious ride to me.

As we began to walk through the park, I remember being surrounded by thousands of people. It was also the hottest day in Texas history, or at least it felt that way. As we were walking, I looked up and saw a ride called The Demon. I'm a pastor's kid, so my first thought was for my mom to pray that thing away. "Come on, Mom, whip out a few Bible verses and let's bring freedom to this theme park," I thought. She reassured me it was just a ride. We continued walking, but I'm still working through the emotional scars that moment left.

I started begging my dad for my favorite treat on the planet: ice cream. I asked over and over again, and my dad kept telling me that we needed to eat "real food" first. Ice cream was very real to me, so I did what any obedient seven-year-old would do in that situation: I asked my mom. Unfortunately, she agreed with my dad and said, "Son, you cannot have ice cream right now." I responded under my breath, without her hearing, "You can't have any ice cream either, Mom."

In the midst of my pity party, I looked to my right and there was a beautiful ice cream stand. Angels were beckoning me, and the sweet taste of chocolate ice cream called to me. I could not overcome the temptation. So I got in line. Yes, I jumped in the ice cream line. Adults around me were giving me confused looks, but I didn't care; I was about to get exactly what I wanted.

When I finally reached the front of the line, the ice cream lady looked at me as I proceeded with my order. After I ordered she asked me, "Where are your parents, little boy?" I said, "Look, ice cream lady, just give me my ice cream." I wasn't saved by grace just yet. When she explained that I owed her money for the order, I realized that I didn't know where my parents were! I needed my parents because who else would pay for this ice cream? Then it really set in: I was lost. I had no clue where my family was. I walked away from the stand and somehow found a security guard in the middle of thousands of people. He grabbed my hand and took me to a lost and found room.

Walking into this room was breathtaking. The AC was ice cold, the couch was supremely comfortable, and a basketball game was on TV. Was this life without parents? I had to admit, it seemed pretty great.

The kid sitting next to me, who was also lost, stood up on the couch, turned around, and looked out the big window behind us. He screamed, "There's my parents! There's my parents! They are riding the train ride!"

I started laughing! Can you imagine the conversation between the couple who lost their child?

"Hey Larry, we lost Jimmy. What should we do?"

"The train ride looks fun. Let's ride that. Jimmy will be fine."

To this day, I'm not sure if Jimmy was reunited with his parents.

As I sat on that couch, it began to sink in. I was lost. And it was my fault. I had done what my dad told me not to do, and now I was in this situation. I thought through every punishment I might receive once I was reunited with my parents. Would I be disowned? Would I be reprimanded and yelled at for my disobedience? Would I be spanked? Would I be in time-out for the rest of my life? Would they take away my Nintendo? I was already condemning myself before I was even found. I was my own judge and jury. I was scared.

I looked outside and I saw my parents running toward the room. My dad led the way. I prepared myself for the worst.

My dad burst through the door and ran straight to me. To my shock, he grabbed me and squeezed me tightly. My arms were at my sides because a hug was not on my list of things that might happen to me.

He pulled back and as I looked in his eyes, I saw he was crying. Wow, did I have this whole moment wrong. With tears streaming down his face, he said something that has always stuck with me. His statement changed my life. Dad said, "Son, I missed you. I love you. Never leave me again." In that moment I had the greatest revelation of my life. I was the one who made the wrong decision. I stood in the wrong line. I functioned in disobedience, and I punished myself before ever giving my dad a chance. I deserved what was coming my way. I deserved the worst. Yet I got love. My dad still loved me.

Yes, Jesus loves you. But let me take this one step further for you. Jesus *still* loves you. While we were still sinners, Christ died (Rom. 5:8). Nails did not keep him on the cross, love did.

We live lives filled with mistakes. We often make wrong decisions and fail to break our sinful cycles. However, God won't stop loving us. That day, I saw my dad differently. What's more, I viewed God differently. I cannot earn or lose his love. His love will chase me down at my worst and love me in my dirt. When I received that picture, I lived *from* love not *for* love.

Right where you are, you are loved. Reading this right now, you are loved. Whatever you did last night, you are loved. He loves you just as you are, and he loves you way too much to keep you that way. When you get a glimpse of real love, it will change you from the inside out. This love will change how you think. This love will change how you live. This love will change how you date. This love will change how you look at your spouse. This love will change how you raise kids. This love will change how you see yourself. This love will change how you walk with God. This love changes everything.

God is speaking to you now, saying, "I miss you. I love you. Never leave me again."

Hosea and Gomer

Before we go any further, let's look at the backstory of Hosea and Gomer. Hosea prophesied around the middle of the eighth century BC, during the tragic final days of the northern king-dom of Israel, and his message is directed primarily to that kingdom. He was the only one of the writing prophets to come from Israel, and though he is identified as the son of Beeri, little else is known about him. His ministry began during or shortly after that of the prophet Amos and lasted for at least thirty-eight years. Amos had prophesied that God would judge Israel at the hands of an unnamed enemy; Hosea identified that enemy as Assyria.[1]

The first three chapters of Hosea tell us about the prophet's family life, which the Lord used as a symbol to illustrate his message to the people of Israel. This is the particular Hosea narrative we will explore together.

If you read through the sixty-six books of the Bible, you will find many stories and references to the love of God. However, one story reveals the immaculate love of God stronger than others, and that is the awkward love story of Hosea and Gomer.

I say awkward because it is like a fairy tale gone wrong. We will go through the entire story later, but first things first. Hosea was a man doing his best to follow God's will for his life. On the flip side, Gomer was a promiscuous woman—a harlot. God was not happy with his people Israel, because they were living in idolatry and abusing the love he had extended toward them. So when God spoke to Hosea and told him to make the first move toward Gomer, things got interesting.

God was not thrilled with the infidelity of his people. Hosea was ready to hear God's voice so he could deliver the message from God's heart. Gomer was living in sin. So naturally, the next move God made was to tell Hosea to marry Gomer.

What! Wait a second. God told a prophet to marry a promiscuous woman? Yes, he sure did. And God explained himself by saying that this shocking union would represent how his people had been unfaithful.

Without hesitation, Hosea married Gomer. There were probably some pretty upset young women who thought Hosea was the one for them. These girls were praying for a ring by spring. Instead, Hosea followed the voice of God and took Gomer as his wife.

I love that this whole story began with Hosea accepting what God said, even though it made no logical sense. If Hosea had stopped for two seconds and thought logically about what God was asking him to do, he most likely would've fought it. This is why you do not let your perception of reality shape God's voice in your life. Rather, you let God's voice shape your reality.

With no further explanation of why God would tell him to marry someone so seemingly incompatible, Hosea went ahead and married her. We do not get a play-by-play of the wedding or what people thought, but I am sure opinions were flying. We do not even get to see what Gomer thought about this series of events. It was Hosea's job to pursue; it was her job to say yes. That is important to remember for later, as this story ends up being much bigger than a love story between a man and a woman.

Hosea took the first step. He made the first move.

Lovestruck

This is how God showed his love among us: He sent his one and only Son into the world that we might live through him. (1 John 4:9 NIV)

Once again, God made the first move. I'm sure you've had moments where you've sat in a room of guilt or regret, wishing you hadn't made that bad decision. All of humanity has been there. What God wants to convey to you and to people across our world is that you did not find love; Love found you.

One of my favorite Michael Jackson songs is "Smooth Criminal." There is just something about MJ's songs that gets you dancing with your no-rhythm self. (I apologize if you feel like you do have rhythm. Actually, I don't . . . you most likely move with passion instead of purpose.) I understand that this is not the most uplifting song in the world, but there is a point to be made.

There is a line in the song where MJ talks about how the person never really saw the crime coming because of how smooth and surprising the criminal acted. This analogy may seem strange to you, but stay with me for a minute. When God sent Jesus as his ultimate showcase of love for us, he became the smoothest criminal of all time. Jesus, full of love and truth, stole death, hell, and the grave away from Satan's grip. He stole the power of sin. He stole the hearts of all those who would relinquish their lives to him. And we never even saw it coming.

God showed his love by sending Jesus. I'm thankful he did not choose a Hallmark card to tell us how much he loved us. Have you ever thought how God could have handled this whole sin and Satan issue? He's God. He has all power and all authority and can do whatever he wants whenever he desires. God didn't send a little love token our way. God sent his own Son. Are you kidding me?

I am a dad and I have sons. I cannot begin to think about sending one of them to be the sacrifice for other people's sin issues. And that is why I am not God. And neither are any of you. Because God did the unthinkable. He sent his very own Son to shake the foundations and create a new world order. What an act of pure love. There is no love comparable to this. God did not want to show his love by taking care of this issue from a distance. God wanted to be an up close and personal God. He didn't just want to tell us; he wanted to show us how "wide and long and high and deep" his love is (Eph. 3:18). And he did this while we were still sinners.

God made the first move. He sent his son Jesus as the greatest love sacrifice in the history of the world. He did it for sinners. He did it for people who would never acknowledge him as Lord and Savior. He did it even for those who curse his name. Jesus died for all of us. Jesus is the smoothest criminal of all time. When the devil thought he defeated Jesus with death, Jesus was defeating death with love.

God found you when you were lost. God saved you when you were stuck. God loves you every step of the way and every breath you take. He made the first move, now you make the next.

JESUS LOVES ME
... THIS I DON'T KNOW

Though our feelings come and go, God's love for us
does not.

C. S. Lewis

What you value the most is what controls you the most.
The way we build our value system directly determines
our quality of life. We do not improve our life by running after
what we deem to be quality or affirming. We do it by living on
and in God's value system.

It is difficult to know God's values when we keep telling him
ours. We want God to give us the values of our heart. We pray
that God will bless us with what we have deemed worthy. We
pray our will over God's will. We ask him to do his work in our
timing. Thus, we become victim to our valueless desires and
miss the invaluable system God wants to set up in our lives.

When we do this, we begin overcompensating for what God
has not given us. We make foolish decisions to get what we never

really needed. We get into relationships for physical reasons because we are lonely. We succumb to divorce because sometimes it seems like the easy way out. We live our life to be liked, only to realize we have incarcerated ourselves in other people's opinions. We've lost our worth.

This is why we do not know that Jesus loves us and why he has no control or effect in us. We are unable to define what is of value, especially when culture inundates us with toxic perspectives and pointless trends. As a result, God's love becomes merely a good thought that changes nothing in our reality.

I knew a young man in high school who had an incredible gift for football. He was so good that he received many Division 1 scholarships and could choose which school he wanted to attend. This young man chose his university carefully because he had aspirations of playing in the NFL. One time when I was putting together a flag football team for a competitive game against some friends, I went to this football star and asked if he would play on my team. He was nice about it but replied, "As much as I would love to, I can't play." When I asked him why, he said something that carried a lot of weight: "I just signed my letter of intent to play Division 1 football. I can't play because what if I get hurt?"

Those last words struck me. This young man knew the difference between a meaningless game and a meaningful one. Why would he risk getting hurt and possibly jeopardizing his bright future for a contest that carried no significance? He knew he could not put himself in harm's way for something that carried no value for his life.

You will refuse to put yourself in danger when you know the value of your life and future. There is so much benefit in knowing your value. How many times do we throw away our future for insignificant moments? How often do we choose immediate pleasures over long-term character and integrity? Once you know the value of your future, you will change the decisions of your present. So how do we find our value?

Gold has great value. I mean real gold, of course, not the fake, knockoff watches and jewelry you can buy from some random guy on a sidewalk. Yes, I fell for that a long time ago. However, I quickly learned that fake gold will turn your skin green if you wear it for very long. It cannot stand the test of time or handle wear and tear like real gold. It is meant to look the part without ever working properly. It has the appearance of real gold but no sustaining worth. You may fool people, but you know that this imitation does not have the same value as real gold.

The Bible talks about gold and its purity. When gold goes through fire, the fire does not destroy it but refines it and reveals its true worth.

> But he knows where I am going. And when he tests me, I will come out as pure as gold. (Job 23:10 NLT)

> These trials will show that your faith is genuine. It is being tested as fire tests and purifies gold—though your faith is far more precious than mere gold. So when your faith remains strong through many trials, it will bring you much praise and glory and honor on the day when Jesus Christ is revealed to the whole world. (1 Peter 1:7 NLT)

It is difficult to accept that value comes from and is revealed in the struggles of life. However, what is God trying to say through verses like these? He is challenging our value system and showing us that we must build our worth on the foundation of faith—not fleeting possessions or shallow pleasures, but the unshakable ground that is the Rock, Jesus Christ.

Faith is where your discovery of real value begins. Accepting that Jesus loves you is how you build your value system. When you know you are loved, you won't settle for the fake version of love. Lust never satisfies, and living loved allows you to walk away from the facade of lust. You will go through storms in life, but your faith and love in Jesus Christ is your ultimate value. Jesus spread his arms on the cross to show you your value. God gave his only Son to show you your worth. Value is not birthed from what you do but the position you are in. Your position as a son or daughter of God is your worth.

You are so loved. That is your meaning in life. You are supremely cared about by God, and he knows your name. You can cling to that when you feel forgotten. When you know your value, you walk and talk differently. You no longer hang around with the same people or in the same places. Your value is not measured by an accolade or achievement; it rests on the firm foundation of Jesus. There is nothing you did to make him start loving you, and there is nothing you can do to make him stop loving you. That is your value. Your life is worth so much—now live like you know that.

The Desensitized Reality

The saying "Jesus loves you" seems cliché. I am not saying that it has lost its power. Not at all. It is one of the most powerful statements a person can say. However, these words do not move the masses like they used to. I think there are many reasons why this statement has lost its zest. It has nothing to do with the statement itself. It has everything to do with the ones receiving the statement.

We are flat-out desensitized as a culture. We are so inundated with information and immorality that we are in the midst of a full-fledged attack on our emotions and spirituality. Everywhere we turn there is sexual temptation. Everyone looks at their phones. We are no longer present-minded. We watch and read about other people more than we live our own lives. We are desensitized by polarizing politics. We are desensitized by TV shows and movies. We are desensitized by constant distractions. This is why it is so difficult to find what is real in a world full of fake.

We're desensitized to the word "love." How many times a day do you say or text the word "love"? I say it all the time! I tell my wife I love her multiple times a day (though I probably need to get better at this because her love language is words of affirmation). I love the free chips and salsa at Mexican restaurants. (So. Good.) I love when there is no traffic. I love coffee. I love sports. I love writing. I love my kids. I love my family. I love Christmas. You get the point, right?

We say "I love you" or "I love this" as easily as we breathe. We watch movies about love. Romance is one of the most popular genres of movies and books today. Have you noticed that if you are watching an action movie, there is a 99 percent chance of a love story being woven into it? People are addicted to this notion of love.

It is in our music. It is laced into every format of entertainment. Love is all around us. Just go to your local mall and watch people; I'm sure you will find teenagers who love publicly displaying their affections for all to see. Because love is so accessible and constantly in our face, we have become desensitized to what love is really supposed to be.

I recently opened my podcast app and typed in the word "love." Selecting the top five search results, I listened for a few hours. I did not look at the sources or voices behind these episodes, but I did catch on that at least two of them were well-known celebrities discussing how to find real love. To spare you from having to do this, let me say it was apparent that a lot of thought goes into love, but a ton more confusion comes out when trying to explain it.

I knew we as a culture struggled to understand what love is, but I never knew our definition was in such dire need of a makeover. I heard discussions that offered no real conclusion on the difference between love and being in love. I listened through one episode that discussed how sex is the best way to find out how you feel about someone else. I even heard a beautiful love story of some couple from the 1950s and how they met; it sounded like a movie. I discovered that no one on these podcasts could sum up love. It is vague and vast. It is either an emotional rush or a crash, depending on the moment. It fills the heart yet also breaks it. It is the single most important resource on the planet, but humanity hasn't quite realized it yet.

We have a culture that wants to define love before we can thoughtfully figure out what it really is. The world will always define love in a way that makes us thirst for a version that only benefits self. There is romantic love, friendship love, love in the form of acceptance, love in the form of being admired, love that idolizes, married love, sibling love—the list goes on and on. No dictionary can give us an accurate definition or synonym for the kind of love we need. The kind of love most people chase after today is a love that is drenched in emotions and wrapped in feelings. However, that version of love will always leave you empty and searching.

If the culture is going to be obsessed with the thought of love, we must become possessed by the truth of it.

Let's look at your Monday through Saturday. Maybe you are a stay-at-home mom, so your life is filled with kid games and kid shows among many other things. Or you could be working full-time and spend hours on end with your coworkers and boss. You could be a college student who is trying to make it from class to class with a passing grade. Whatever your life looks like for these six days, you just spent 144 hours being immersed in your surroundings. And remember, most of our surroundings include people infatuated with this idea of love: 144 hours of life lived around certain people and beliefs; 144 hours to buy into doubts and insecurities; 144 hours to struggle through and barely make it out.

Then on Sunday morning you decide to go to church. And in church that Sunday, your pastor gets up for about thirty to forty minutes and talks about the Bible and Jesus. And in this particular sermon, the pastor says, "Jesus loves you!" As you sit there and hear the words, you remain unmoved. You may think, "How will that change my life? How does that get the laundry done? Doesn't this preacher have something more revelatory to say?" You struggle to find how your reality is impacted by a love you think you know. You've become numb to this love. You can feel your emotions, just not God's love.

One of the main reasons we miss God's love is because we are looking for a feeling when God's love is a truth. Maybe you don't feel anything when you hear that Jesus loves you. However, it changes you when it becomes a truth. You have to choose daily to know that he loves you and will never leave you. This is why a pastor's thirty-minute sermon on Sunday cannot be your spiritual filling for the week. Rather, it is your encouragement to go get this love that is at your fingertips.

You spent 144 hours living your life, and guess what? That one-hour church service barely moved you. Not because the worship experience was lacking, but because you were already filled with a desensitized cultural outlook on life. The longer you listen to a desensitized culture, the more you fail to see what is real in the midst of fake.

Consider how you spend your days. Your Monday through Saturday does not have to be the same as it has always been. You can break through on a Wednesday afternoon. You can still praise strong on a Monday morning. You can live in the truth of love every day that you choose.

Just because you do not feel this real love does not mean it is not with you and for you. The biggest mistake we make is to look for a different answer to a problem that God has already solved. Don't get me wrong; God's love is not emotionless. In fact, once you decide it is a truth in your life, you will have powerful, life-changing encounters with his love. I can remember moments in my life when I was absolutely floored by the love of God. But this love is bigger than one encounter. There is an encounter for you every day in this love. You are loved with an everlasting love.

More than ever before we need people on this planet living loved.

> "Israel, out looking for a place to rest, met GOD out looking for them!" GOD told them, "I've never quit loving you and never will. Expect love, love, and more love!" (Jer. 31:2–3)

Expect love! Seriously, start expecting that it is in you, with you, and sustaining you. God's love for you is good and will produce good things through you. I have come to realize we receive to the level we expect. You will receive God's love to the same extent as you expect that love to help you and fulfill you.

Most likely you have a boss. That boss signs your paycheck, and you know exactly when that check is supposed to show up. If that check is one day late, you hunt down the person who has stolen your money or you call your employer to ask what happened. You do this because you are expecting your check to be in your account at a certain time. You know exactly when you are to be in possession of your hard-earned paycheck.

What if we brought that same intensity and expectancy to seeing God's love in our lives? Every day is payday with God, but we often fail to communicate with the Boss to get all that he has waiting for us. He wants to lavish his love on you. He wants to radically challenge your perspective with this love. Expect more love, all the time. When you don't feel it, don't compensate by making an ill-advised decision. Maybe God is testing you to see who you will run to when you need something to gratify your soul. You receive God's love to the extent you expect his love. It's time to receive his love in a manner like never before. It is time to expect that God is your all in all and that his love changes everything.

Love Kills Hate

Many people do not know Jesus loves them because of the intense hate that persists around the world. Hate is swiftly making its move among us, and if we do not step up soon, hate will continue to grow.

Hate is nothing new and exists in many forms, yet we seem surprised by this. Hate comes in the shape of religious beliefs, racial prejudices, social backgrounds, politics—basically any ideology you can think of. Hate is being peddled to the masses as the newest trend when it's been a scheme of darkness for centuries.

The name Satan means "accuser," and he is known as "the accuser of our brethren" (Rev. 12:10 NKJV). One of the devil's main goals is not just to steal our faith but to divide our hearts. Division is a branch that grows on this sinful tree of hate. Satan hates everything and everyone.

Martin Luther King Jr. once said so eloquently, "I have decided to stick with love. Hate is too great a burden to bear."[2] And hate *is* a burden. I am not even talking about the "big" forms of hate that you may find it easy to refrain from. What about more subtle kinds of hatred? These can come through offense, disagreement, financial inequality, or even just disliking how another person leads their life. I believe the small windows of hate that we leave open lead us to the places we thought we would never be.

Love is a choice. The fact that hate exists does not steal away the power that Jesus loves you. The moment you begin to believe in this insane love of Jesus, hate will be absolutely disgusting to you. You cannot celebrate division when you are united in this great love.

Here is a simple yet healthy test for you to try: Think about a specific person. If you feel any form of disdain toward them in your heart, you may need a refreshing of love. I am not saying you cannot dislike something or someone, but if some deep offense rises in you, you aren't healthy.

Love grows but so does hate. Hate never starts big; it begins with small whispers and disagreements. What you feed the most will flourish. It is time to flip the script on hate and show ourselves and this world that real love does exist. And real love will change whatever it touches, including hate.

Pressure to Impress No One

There is a pressure that surrounds all of us. We feel it at a consistent rate, most of the time on a daily basis. It is difficult to define and just as hard to ignore. We often do not know whether it is healthy or not. Nor do we know whether it comes from God or from within ourselves. It is the pressure to impress, to be something we are not and look good for people who are not watching. It is the pressure to keep up with other people's status. It is the pressure to be more, do more, and have more at younger ages than ever before. It is the pressure that gets us in a rush to go where we have no directions. It is the pressure that a mom feels to have her house in perfect order and her kids behaving better. It is the pressure that steals our gratitude and substitutes discontentment. It is the pressure that causes you to live above your means because you have not learned how to act your wage. It is the pressure in ministry to have the biggest church in your city, your state, or even the country. It is the pressure to be well received and gain influence while measuring your success by social media. It is the pressure to perform for your boss, to be a great Christian in the eyes of others, and to keep up with a life God has not yet given you the grace for.

The most valuable thing you can do is to run at the pace God sets and not try to speed that up. The moment you attempt to outpace God, you start feeling this unnecessary pressure. I believe pressure can be very important for growth in life and as a believer. Pressure can pull the best out of you, especially in intense moments, but only when it causes you to trust that God will come through because of the opportunity in front of you. The pressure to impress no one, however, will drag you down.

Your goal should not be to impress but to submit. When you are fully submitted to the ways and will of God, you will be impressive. But you will be impressive not because of what you strive for but what you are living in. Let the following statement free you of the burden you have been carrying: You have nothing to lose and nothing to prove.

Let me say that again for all my speed readers. You have nothing to lose and nothing to prove!

This statement changed my life and it can change yours too. It is founded in the loving heart of Jesus, because with God you have nothing to lose and nothing to prove. You do not need to live your life in the fear of what you might lose. You do not need to live one more day in the chains of a perspective that is causing you to live a safe life. You cannot lose with God, because he has never lost! And what you think is losing, God may call learning. Or as I like to say, "You don't win some and lose some . . . you win some and learn some." Lead your life in the love of God and you will see that you have nothing to lose.

You also have nothing to prove. This pressure to impress no one is a rampant disease that is taking over our hearts and minds. You have nothing to prove to your social media followers. You have nothing to prove to people who believe you should be further ahead in life.

You do need to live up to the call of God on your life, but that is a process. And while you are in this process, you don't have to prove to anyone what God spoke in your spirit. God is the one who can piece your life together and make you stand out. You can literally or figuratively shout and jump for people to notice you, yet it seems to fail every time. Why? Because God wants you to be content in his presence before you arrive at his promise.

Jesus loves you, this you do know. At least now you do. Whatever is holding you back, release it and live for the audience of One. And from here on out, when you hear the statement "Jesus loves you," let it move you and challenge you to always live and abide in this everlasting love.

UNLOVED

The nature of God's love is unchangeable. Ours alternates all too readily. If it is our habit to love God with our own affection we shall turn cold towards Him whenever we are unhappy.

Watchman Nee

Hosea put it well: I'll call nobodies and make them somebodies; I'll call the unloved and make them beloved.

Romans 9:25

I love coffee. No, I really love coffee. One day, as I was sitting in a trendy coffee shop and writing this book while drinking a phenomenal French-press coffee, a couple millennial-age girls sat right behind me. I am not the nosy type who eavesdrops on other people's conversations. However, they were talking at a level the whole place could hear, and I did catch a few sentences from their conversation before I put my headphones on.

They were talking about relationships and love—a very interesting combination as I was writing about the boundless and fulfilling love of God. The one girl said to her friend, "I just want a relationship." (You know where this is headed.) She continued, "I don't want commitment, just a boyfriend. Someone who would comfort me and come over when I am having a bad day." Now, I guarantee this conversation happens all the time, all over the world. And I do not necessarily think this girl had bad or evil intentions. Nevertheless, her desire points out that our world has an epidemic of living unloved.

I lived unloved for most of my life. Yes, I had great parents who loved me and did everything possible for me to be successful in life. Yes, I had two older sisters who, despite the jokes and pranks, loved me. Yes, I had friends in my life who brought value to my world. Sure, I had the occasional girlfriend here and there. So it was not like my life was void of relationships.

By now you are probably wondering what I mean by living unloved, right? You are thinking to yourself, "Those sound like some good ingredients to produce love in your life. You have family, friends, and relationships. Why in the world would you feel unloved?" I asked myself that same question for many years.

I always felt like something was missing, even when all my relationships were solid. I found myself making irrational decisions that contradicted what I was taught from the Bible. I found myself trying to fill this unexplainable void with the poison of pornography. I thought that by doing more of what

I desired, I would eventually reach total satisfaction. I was unloved, and I thought I was incurable.

See, I was unloved in church services. I grew up in church, sleeping on the front pew every Sunday until my parents would not let me take church naps any longer at the ripe age of twenty-one. (Joking. Sort of.) I had heard every sermon and leadership talk possible. And let me tell you, my parents are extremely gifted pastors, so it wasn't like our church was boring or irrelevant. In fact, our church was passionate and fully alive.

Church was where I learned how to worship. Church was also where I saw the most judgmental Christians.

Church was where I saw hundreds and thousands of people give their hearts to Christ in such beautiful altar call moments. Church was also where I saw people hiding behind facades and wearing church clothes that were cleaner than their character.

Church was where I witnessed God provide miracles to the needy and hope to the hopeless. Church was also where I attended funerals of people who had been asking God for healing.

Church was where I met Jesus. Church was also where I became numb.

See, like many of you, I had great church attendance. And I encourage church attendance because I believe we need to go to grow. We all need a healthy community. However, I pray that church becomes more than a moral obligation on your spiritual checklist. Attendance is not what opens you up to the Spirit. *How* you attend is what determines what you will receive.

I try to give myself grace, since I was young when I was just a weekly attendee. I had so much to process as a young believer:

Why did people leave our church for another and then gossip about my parents when all Mom and Dad were doing was loving people? How could people who say they love God be so cruel? How do people who claim to be saved by grace have so little of it to give? I was hurt and confused. But those weren't my real issues. I was living unloved.

I went to a Christian school up until my freshman year of high school. Surely a school that has "Christian" in its name should be full of like-minded believers. In my experience, that was not the case. I appreciate how many vulgar, unsaved kids were at a school where we were allowed to have chapels and classes about God. However, little ol' church kid me did not fully understand what was going on. So there I was again, trying to find myself in a world that loves to define people. Even through my years at a Christian school, I lived unloved.

I tried relationships. I attempted to address this strange void I felt even though I believed in God. That's just it, right? You can be a Christian and still live with a void. You can be a believer in God and still live unloved.

I pray that you can see I am not bitter about any of my past experiences. In fact, I believe my past experiences have allowed me to see clearer and lean into God's grace more than I ever have before. But what are we to do with a society filled with hopelessness? What are we to do as believers when we know about God and know God but still feel unloved?

I went to college on a football scholarship, and it was my first time living away from my parents. I was excited and nervous. For the first time, I got away from my comfortable church bubble. And it proved to be the best thing in the world for my life.

In college I got to a point where I was pretty empty. I was tired. I was worn out. I was making dangerous decisions and following hazardous feelings. I dealt with a bout of depression as a freshman. "What's the point of my life?" is something I would often think to myself. There are no age limits on depression and living unloved.

I remember getting so fed up that I gave God a chance. Imagine that—as a young man who believed God was real, I had never actually given God my full life and complete control. I had only given him the areas I was comfortable with him knowing about, even though God knew every part of me. This too seems to be a common occurrence among Christians.

So with years of church experience under my belt, I decided to get on my knees and see whether God could do something better with my life than how I was handling it. I'll never forget that moment of surrender. A sweet sense of his presence filled the whole room. God lifted a burden off my shoulders. And guess what? For the first time in my life, I felt loved. Different from the love my parents gave me. Different from what a relationship with another person could give. For the first time ever, I felt an overwhelming love beyond words. It was the real love of Jesus Christ. I had been saved, but now I knew I was loved. And not because God had failed to love me all those years. No, I had been the one who failed to receive the love that God was constantly trying to release over my life.

I wish I could tell you my life instantly changed. I wish I could tell you that everything magically got better. In fact, the attacks came a little stronger. God's love does not make things easier, but it does make things possible. Because I accepted this real love that the world just could not give, I could walk full of faith through every storm. With this real love, I could walk through trials with a smile on my face. With this kind of love, I knew nothing could stop me.

When you live unloved, you are constantly searching for something God has already given to you. The reason you are so tired is because you are working hard to fill your void. To find real love, you do not have to do more for others or for God. Real love does not come from the arms of another imperfect human. Real love does not come from people liking and complimenting you. Real love does not even come from getting exactly what you want, when you want. Real love is found only in the arms of God.

Learn to be loved. You are God's beloved, so guess what? Be loved. Sin won't satisfy what only love can fill.

Baby Names

I remember when my wife and I were naming each of our boys. Names are important because children have to live with them for the rest of their lives. We ruled out any name from a person in our past we didn't like. We would not name our children after ex-boyfriends or third-grade bullies. (Don't judge us, you do it too.) Baby names are big decisions.

God took the reins when it came to naming Hosea and Gomer's kids: he called their oldest son Jezreel, their daughter Lo-Ruhamah, and their youngest son Lo-Ammi. As you might guess, these names didn't end up on the list of popular baby names for that year. Or any year for that matter.

Let's dig into the meanings of these names before we shrug them off as strange-sounding Old Testament words. When God names something or someone, it is on purpose and for a purpose. In this case, God used the children's names to send a message to the people of Israel. A bit of a hidden message, but a strong one nonetheless.

The name Jezreel sounds like a nice, typical Old Testament name, but it comes from a massacre that took place in the land of Jezreel (2 Kings 10:1–11). God's punishment was to break the people of Israel because of what happened in the Valley of Jezreel. So the name of Hosea's firstborn son pointed to how undisciplined the people of Israel had been and God's coming punishment on them. Sweet. Great start to the baby names.

Next up, we have the popular girl's name Lo-Ruhamah. You know a few baby Lo-Ruhamahs, right? God chose this name for Hosea's only daughter, and it means "no mercy" or "unloved." God was fed up with how his people were acting, and this name spoke of his plan to deprive Israel of real love.

Hosea and Gomer's youngest son was named Lo-Ammi. If you say this one fast you can maybe get away with it sounding almost normal. Lo-Ammi means "not my people." Basically, God called him "disowned." That would not go over well on the playground for little Lo.

So God named Hosea's children "undisciplined," "deprived," and "disowned." And this was God's message to Israel: they had been acting undisciplined, deprived, and disowned for a long time, and he was not having any more of it. Now, as we know, God was revealing the nature of Israel's disobedience; he was not actually leaving them. He wouldn't leave them. He loved them too much. However, God was unhappy with how they were behaving. They were living like they were unloved. They had yet to figure out that the real love of God was all they needed.

Undisciplined, deprived, and disowned—the names of Hosea and Gomer's children accurately depict how unloved people lead their lives. Have you ever noticed, possibly in your own actions, how people often do shocking things? We cannot find real love because we allow ourselves to be led by feelings. We don't recognize real love because we are searching for an emotion. Rather than living in a way that shows we believe Jesus loves us, we do shocking things because we think that God's love is not enough.

Unloved people tend to be undisciplined. When we have no foundation of authentic love, we will fall for the first thing that remotely resembles something real. This is why we buy magazines that tell about the latest celebrity hookups and breakups. This is why we watch a movie and wish our marriage was more like that of the couple on-screen. We run to anything that may give us a quick fix for the longing of our souls. We run back to old relationships. We run to pornography. We think happiness might be found in a different marriage. We follow an old high school sweetheart on social media and hold on to a soul tie from our lack of discipline. Unloved people cannot muster up discipline because it is difficult for them to discern what is real or fake anymore. Discipline can only come from the confidence of genuine love.

Unloved people are also deprived people, and deprived people are thirsty people. People depriving themselves of God's love live from a place where they are trying to quench their own thirst with their own desires. Let's get one thing straight: we are deprived of God's love not because of anything he does, but as a result of following our wants instead of his ways. This lifestyle leads us to a place where it is difficult to trust ourselves. What we think we need is not actually what we need; it is just what we want. What we want becomes defiled by our desire to feel satisfied. And what God wants for us is nearly impossible to identify because it looks nothing like the answer we are after. Living deprived of what we need leaves us bound to what we want.

> Don't be naive. There are difficult times ahead. As the end approaches, people are going to be self-absorbed, money-hungry, self-promoting, stuck-up, profane, contemptuous of parents, crude, coarse, dog-eat-dog, unbending, slanderers, impulsively wild, savage, cynical, treacherous, ruthless, bloated windbags, addicted to lust, and allergic to God. They'll make a show of religion, but behind the scenes they're animals. Stay clear of these people. (2 Tim. 3:1–5)

This passage is a strong and clear explanation of how deprived people end up. God is not depriving us of his love; we are depriving ourselves from receiving it. This is the message God sent to the people of Israel in Hosea's day and it is the message he is sending to us. You no longer need to live in the cycles of sin or on the carousel of addiction. Often our greatest addiction is not a substance but acceptance. Humanity is fighting to find its place. We search for our identity, yet we will never find who we are in the desert of desires.

Deprivation of real love can lead to depression. Deprivation can bring you to dangerous decisions. Deprivation may be the very thing that causes you to reject where God is bringing you because it does not make sense to your soul. Your soul longs to be accepted. Acceptance is not found at the bottom of a bottle or even in a healthy marriage. Jesus is the answer to the thirsty heart.

Finally, unloved people are disowned people. God's message to Israel was that they were no longer his people. They had chosen to become disconnected from God, thus finding themselves with no authority. Disowned carries a few meanings, but the main one is rejection. However, the tables are turned here. It is not the people but God who feels disowned. God is looking at his people with love and feeling like they want nothing to do with him. Since the people of Israel have chosen to disown God, they have to deal with the aftermath of that decision.

Disowned people are disconnected. Disowned people become their own authority and their own god. They view their theology and thinking as the best way and the right way. Disowned people appear put together, like everything in their life is good. In reality, no one knows how they are doing because they do not feel like anyone cares. They feel like nothing will help them. Disowned people use Scripture out of context to try and prove to others that their life is on track. Disowned people eventually become owned by what gives them the quickest fill.

Disowned people are posting on social media, trying to impress followers who don't care. Disowned people are out to get attention from others who are not looking. We are living disowned from our original Owner. God created us in his image, yet here we are as a society, acting crazy and blaming it on how we were raised. Your disadvantage in life was never meant to lead you to living disowned.

As the story of Hosea and Gomer begins to unfold, we'll discover there is hope for the undisciplined, deprived, and disowned heart. I encourage you to do an inventory of your actions and see if you are living in a manner that shouts "unloved" to the world. The truth is that you are so loved, and it is time to take the love of Jesus more seriously than we ever have before.

> I will show love to those I called "Not loved." And to those I called "Not my people," I will say, "Now you are my people." And they will reply, "You are our God!" (Hosea 2:23 NLT)

THE IMAGE MIRAGE

What comes into our minds when we think about God is the most important thing about us.

A. W. Tozer

What is love? Love takes on a million different meanings and can evoke a million different emotions. But what does it mean?

> Whoever does not love does not know God, because God is love. (1 John 4:8 NIV)

Well, that was easy. The Bible just dropped it on us in a powerfully clear way. God is love. Nevertheless, as simple as that is to type, it is not so simple to grasp. If everyone comprehended this verse correctly, no one would have an identity crisis.

We learn from this verse that God *is* love. We may think that God has love. But if we take a closer look, we see that Scripture is clear: God does not just have love or give love. God *is* love. He is the embodiment of love. He is the foundation of love. And the proof of this great love is Jesus.

That's why our definition of love matters. It usually starts with how we were raised. Maybe you were raised in a broken home. Maybe you feel like you are the product of a divorce. Maybe you can't shake past abuse that was unfairly a part of your upbringing. Maybe you are still in a marriage or relationship where infidelity has taken place.

What if I told you that our definition of love has been tainted by the skeletons in our closets? We all have them. We all have our secret things that nobody knows about us except for us. The problem is that our past becomes the framework in which we define love. It also shapes how we begin to define God and who he is. Yes, you can bring your brokenness to God, but do not view God through your brokenness. That is how you come to blame him for your hurts.

God is love. Hindsight will reveal to you that God was not distant in your worst moments. He has been right there with you every step of the way. Life and people may have forsaken you, but do not let someone's broken image cause you to doubt God's character. If you are looking for love from God, stop asking him to give it to you. He already has. Start walking in God's love now that you know he is the ultimate foundation of love.

Measurements

When I got married, I remember going to get my suit fitted. I recall how the tailor brought out a measuring tape and began to measure different places on my body. Nobody warned me about this. I had this man, whose name I did not know, measuring me as he pleased. He seemed confident, so I didn't stop him from doing his job.

I didn't think about it until afterward, but he measured my body so I could get the best-fitting suit possible. I mean, I was flattered at first, but then I realized how necessary it was for him to get my specific measurements. Once I got my suit, I knew my wife would love it. It was perfectly tailored to my physique.

How ridiculous would it have been for me to turn down this custom-fit suit and borrow my friend's suit to wear for my wedding? It would have made absolutely no sense. Of course I wore the suit that had been tailor-made for me, not someone else.

However, this happens all the time when it comes to our callings. Every person reading this has a purpose to fulfill in life. You have a calling from God. Not everyone is living in this God-given calling, but everyone does have one. The breakdown begins when we take our tailor-made, perfectly measured calling and compare it to someone else's. This is when we get into trouble. Just ask David.

> Then Saul outfitted David as a soldier in armor. He put his bronze helmet on his head and belted his sword on him over the armor. David tried to walk but he could hardly budge. David told Saul, "I can't even move with all this stuff on me. I'm not used to this." And he took it all off. (1 Sam. 17:38–39)

David was being told what to wear. This happens all the time. I have personally experienced it when people wanted me to fit with their view of me. I would begin to listen to people's opinions about what I should do and where I should go, and I felt trapped. I felt limited by their words. However, it seemed easier to keep wearing everyone's opinions than to face my real, broken self. And at least I had people who were on my side—although only so long as I fit into their measurements for my life.

Since I was a pastor's kid, everyone had a hope and plan for my life. I was an easy target with my parents running a growing, thriving church. I got so lost in other people's intentions that I could not discern what I really wanted for my life. I allowed people's opinions and approval to become my measurements for success. I eventually found my way out, but we must be careful to not love a compromised calling because of other people. People who do not love you should not be able to speak into you. And if their words did not make you, remember that their words cannot break you.

Social media is another measurement where we unconsciously conform to molds and measurements of what people think. No matter which social media platform we use, there is an epidemic of insecurity plaguing our posts. For every picture we post, we use dozens of filters to enhance the photo. We then wait to see if anyone will like or approve of what we just posted. If everyone loves that particular post, we think that version of ourselves must be best. We keep putting on armor that does not fit in order to please others.

In fact, every time we get a like or comment on social media, dopamine is released in the brain. Dopamine is a chemical associated with pleasure. It is partly responsible for addictions because the brain tells us to go back to whatever gave us such an intense, pleasurable feeling. The way dopamine is released in the brain during drug use is the same way it is released when we check social media and receive responses. We must be careful how far we allow ourselves to go on this technology platform or we will find ourselves trying to impress people who do not even care.

It is time to stop wearing armor that was not made for you. You do not have to fit into the words spoken over you. You do not have to conform to the intentions of other people. You do not need to carry yourself in a manner that is not true to God's perfect calling for your life.

David complied with Saul's wishes and put on armor that did not fit. The Bible even says that David tried to walk around in it, but he could not function. You may not be able to function properly in your calling and in God's love because you are still wearing your past. Wearing your past will wear you out. You have been trying to move forward but it seems like you cannot go anywhere fast. Sometimes it seems logical to hold on to that past memory, past hurt, or unhealed wound. It seems appropriate because being a victim becomes addicting. We want people to feel bad for us and give us constant encouragement because we always paint ourselves as the worst situation in the room.

What would have happened if David went out and fought Goliath in Saul's armor? If he failed, he could have blamed it on the armor he was wearing and how he did not have good mobility. He would have been a victim of what he allowed to be placed on himself. You do not have to live life with this unbearable weight, hoping that other people will show sympathy to you. Remember dopamine? That also gets released when we receive sympathy and empathy. If you are in a Christian environment, there will be a season where people are sympathetic toward you. However, you are not called to stay bound with chains that are meant to be broken. Sympathy is nice, but it will end. Healing is a much better way. In fact, healing is the only way to move forward. You do not need to wait for anyone's approval to throw off what has been stopping you from going to the next level.

Our limitations often come in the form of comparison. David refused to live by someone else's measurements. He was not willing to conform to those limitations. I'm sure plenty of soldiers would have been honored to wear King Saul's armor, but David did not need it because he already had his own armor. No, not literal armor, but David knew that what he had was all he needed.

> Then David took his shepherd's staff, selected five smooth stones from the brook, and put them in the pocket of his shepherd's pack, and with his sling in his hand approached Goliath. (1 Sam. 17:40)

David took his staff, which had helped him defeat previous foes, his shepherd's pack, and his sling. David didn't need anything from anyone else to be used in a mighty way by God. He knew who he was. He knew who had his back. When you know who you are, you will refuse to conform.

David could have looked around and realized that everyone had a sword while he only had a sling. Instead, the very thing he already possessed was what God used to defeat the giant.

Don't question whether God can use you. Instead, question whether you are trying to fit into measurements and limitations that do not belong to you.

This is an image issue at heart. David knew whose image he was made in, so he could easily reject anything that would compromise that image. Today, we have an identity crisis. We cannot fully receive the real love of God until we address our image issues.

Back to the Start

From the beginning of our existence, image has been a big deal. Starting in Genesis 1, the Bible takes us on a journey of how God created the universe in six days and, like a boss, rested on the seventh day. There are some intriguing and revealing ways God goes about creating, so let's look deeper into Genesis 1.

In Genesis 1, God masterfully created the heavens and the earth. He painted the sky with stars and hung the sun and moon perfectly in their places. God then created fish and birds in an intriguing way:

> Then God said, "Let the waters swarm with fish and other life. Let the skies be filled with birds of every kind." (Gen. 1:20 NLT)

Straightforward, right? Let's look at this from a different point of view.

God did not speak to the fish to become fish. Of course he would not do that, because there were no fish to speak to. Instead, God spoke to the waters and said, "Let the waters swarm with fish." In essence, he spoke to the environment that the fish would need to sustain their life.

Then he created the birds. Once again he did not just tell the birds to come to life and start flying around. God strategically said, "Let the skies be filled with birds of every kind." God spoke to the environment that the birds would need to sustain their life.

God spoke to the water to create fish. He then spoke to the sky to create birds. The pattern here is that God spoke to the source in which the animal would live, thrive, move, and breathe. Fish cannot stay alive outside of their aquatic environment. Birds need air for life and flight. So if God spoke to the source to create these creatures, to what did he speak to create humans?

> Then God said, "Let us make human beings in our image, to be like us." (Gen. 1:26 NLT)

God spoke to the waters for the creation of fish. God spoke to the skies for the creation of birds. God spoke to himself for the creation of humans. Just like fish cannot survive without the water, just like birds cannot survive without air, you and I cannot survive without our source—almighty God.

God wants you to know from the very beginning that you have a source and that you have been made in his image. God is the source of life and love. He is the source you run to when you are in need. Outside of God we have no hope and no life. How beautiful that the beginning of humanity points directly back to a loving God.

God created us in his image. He knew that we would have an image problem in our time—of course he knew. And if we would just go back to the start and look at how we were created, we would see that we are already crafted and put together in the image in which we are called to live. God did not create us according to an image that was imperfect or broken; he created us in his own perfect image. This does not mean we are perfect people. It means that God did not make a mistake with us. From the beginning we were created in the image of a relational, loving God. This is why you do not need another relationship in your life if you are looking for hope and an identity. Those things are only found in Jesus Christ. We were created for relationship, specifically relationship with our heavenly Father.

First John 4:8 tells us that God is love. You were made in the image of God, so when you look in the mirror, you see someone crafted with perfect love. When you degrade yourself with negative thoughts, you tear down the perfect image of love. You do not need anyone to tell you that they love you in order to have hope or feel loved. You are the walking proof that God's love is present. You are a living example of what God's love looks like on this earth. You have been intricately and beautifully crafted from the image of real love. God loves you more than you know. And if you do not believe me, then realize that he gives you your next breath. He gives you grace that will cover you. He did not make you from something ugly or unacceptable. You are made in the image of perfect love himself.

And how much does God love you? Here is how much God loves you: Jesus. Jesus was not sent to save us *from* the Father but to save us *for* the Father. John 3:16 paints a beautiful picture that God's ultimate plan to redeem humanity is driven by his undeniable, relentless love for you: "For God so loved the world that he gave his one and only Son." You are worth God's only Son.

The dictionary defines a mirage as "something illusory, without substance or reality." Too often we find ourselves chasing an image mirage that has no substance or reality. We try to wear other people's opinions, only to realize that's the wrong measurement for our lives. Stop running after what you think you see and start running after what you know. Don't chase an image mirage. Chase the Image Maker, Jesus Christ.

WHEN YOUR PAST BECOMES YOUR PRESENT

The very first step toward change is to believe that you can. You don't have to stay the way you are because God is a God of change and transformation. He can bring change to your life and bring the best out of you.

Brian Houston

There is a full-fledged assault against this love of Jesus. For sure it is attacked by things like lust and rejection, but also by distraction. Many of us right now battle between fighting for love in the present or running back to highlights of the past. I say "highlights" because when we look back at the past, we often see only the pleasures without the pain. This is what the devil wants us to do: romanticize our past while demonizing our present, thus crippling our future.

Weigh your present pain versus your past pleasure. Your past is not better than where God is trying to take you. Your present questions will not be answered by returning to what God brought you out of. No more negotiating at the table of compromise. Let your past build you, not define you.

As strong and true as some of those statements are, it is so much easier said than done. Our past has a strong pull on us. Some people have conquered their past, of course, but we would not be human if we didn't admit that sometimes it just feels right to go back. This is why we must be spiritually sober while exploring the depths of where we came from. However, if we do not walk away from our past, we will walk right back into it. This is exactly what happened to Gomer.

Hosea, Gomer, and their three children were living their happily ever after. They had a new life, a family, and God in control. It all sounds like a dream, right? But sometimes when everything seems to be OK, that's when the enemy attacks. Except the attack is not always from the enemy. Sometimes the attack comes from things we have yet to leave behind or heal from. For Gomer, it came from her past.

Gomer was a prostitute when God told Hosea to marry her. To go from prostitute to prophet's wife is quite the turnaround of lifestyles. The Bible doesn't tell us a lot about Gomer's next move, but we read in Hosea 3 that she was unfaithful to Hosea and returned to her past life. This is shocking because surely her marriage was a much better situation than the life of a prostitute. Nonetheless, when a person's mind has not been renewed, they live on the edge of their past.

I think Gomer hoped a new situation would take away old demons. I fully believe she had every intention of being true to Hosea. But we learn that it takes more than good intentions to live faithfully. Intentions that never materialize end up demoralizing the will to change. It is possible that Gomer got to a place where walking back seemed like the only logical answer for her. How? Because a mind without God is a mind without hope.

Have you gotten to this place before? The place where sin looks logical and your past becomes attractive? We learn from Gomer that no standard or way of life can bring the freedom that only the love of Jesus brings. On the outside, she had it all together. On the inside, it seems there was a daily battle that she never addressed.

God will not heal what you hide. You cannot kill what you won't confront. You do not have to live one decision away from your past the rest of your life.

It's possible that Gomer had become numb. She loved her kids. She loved her husband. But maybe she did not fully realize how loved she was. Not by her kids or her husband but by God.

This is a clear indication that we must not place anything ahead of Jesus on our priority list. Jesus should not just be first on your list; he should be intertwined into every part of your life. It is not Jesus and then everything else. It is Jesus and your family. Jesus and your spouse. Jesus and your work. Jesus and your dreams. Jesus and your hobbies. Jesus in everything is how our lives should look. It is not only that Jesus is first; Jesus is in all aspects of your world.

If Jesus exists only at the top of your priority list, it is common for there to be areas God has no control over. Jesus can be first, but you can still struggle with lust. You know he is Lord of all, but lust still has its way with your mind. You can believe in Jesus but still live in compromise. It is time to bring Jesus into every area of your priority list. Jesus can break every chain; however, he cannot break the chains you never give him.

We all have a past. A great start for unity among humanity would be for everyone to admit we have our own stories and journeys. The landscape of life looks different for each of us, but we are who we are today because of who we were or where we came from. Gomer appeared to have walked away from her past. If anyone knew she was thinking about leaving a great situation, I'm sure someone, maybe Hosea, would have pulled her aside for a life-altering conversation. But no one else can help what they do not see or hear.

I understand God was using the story of Hosea and Gomer to illustrate his relationship with Israel, but there is something he wants us to learn from it too. We cannot act mature on the outside while still being haunted on the inside by choices from our teenage years.

Are you really free? Have you really walked away? Or are you premeditating your next sinful move as you go to church and lead your outwardly Christian life? There is more to life than this. Your past cannot define you if you don't let it.

I think good can come from looking back at where you came from and how much you've been through. Life is not a competition to have the greatest testimony. Nonetheless, you can extract some good from hindsight.

Hindsight can build your faith and teach you wisdom that no podcast could give. Looking back at your past can show you that you are doing better than you think and are further along than you realize. Looking back can reveal God's goodness to pull you out of some dumb mistakes. Hindsight can teach you that success is not about how far you go but how far you've come.

Some of you need to hear this: you are already successful. What you are striving for may be an illusion based on how you define success. Success is not an income. Success is not influence-based. Success means doing all you can with what you have. You have come too far to give up now. And today's success will look different than where God will call you in the coming seasons of life. Each day you wake up, you have been given a gift. Today is the day the Lord has made. What will you do with this day that God tailor-made for you? Your past failures need to become your present lessons so you can avoid the pitfalls that once got the best of you.

You can't stop here. You can't quit now. There is too much riding on your life to walk away from all that God has done and is doing. There is a plan for your life. You may be like Gomer and not see what God is doing. But please do not take the Gomer way out and return to what look like satisfying pleasures. It is time to divorce your past because you have a calling to fulfill.

Can you imagine when Hosea got home that day and found Gomer missing? It's almost as if God quickened Hosea's spirit to know where she went. What a difficult situation for him. He had obeyed God and now was walking in heartache because of an unfaithful wife. Saying yes to God does not protect us from pain, but we can be confident that God will never leave us when we are in the midst of it.

When Your Past Meets Praise

> Enter into his gates with thanksgiving, and into his courts with praise: be thankful unto him, and bless his name. (Ps. 100:4 KJV)

This verse gives us directions for getting to the place we need to live. We often guide our lives while hoping God is in the car with us as we drive. This is how we get ourselves into places where we need God to bail us out. But there is a better way to live. There are new directions to take for your life.

The first thing to realize about your past is how easy it is to get there. All you have to do is take a U-turn and you are back where you started. But there is a remedy for this: praise. That sounds way too simple, right? It does to me. I thought there would be a nine-step process to destroying the past. If you are trying to avoid your past, you are spending your energy on the wrong fight. Your freedom does not come from trying to avoid something but from engaging with someone. That someone is Jesus.

Thankfulness is the first way to enter his gates. I love that thankfulness comes first because that is often the very thing we lack the most. It is hard to be thankful when nothing is going your way. It is difficult to find thankful words about something that is painful in your life. That is why God challenges us to look higher than the situation in front of us.

Thankfulness is a key that will unlock blessings in your life. More importantly, thankfulness will lead you to the Blesser. When you learn to thank God for who he is, you will not be worried about what you lack, because you will see his majesty. Thankfulness is the foundation to worship that breaks through. So find reasons to be thankful. If it is difficult, go back to the fact that God woke you up today. And as long as you are still breathing, you still have a purpose. Maybe Gomer was one of those people who could not find much to be thankful about. Thus, worship was not a part of her warfare. Let's learn from this and see that thankfulness brings us into God's presence.

Psalm 100:4 says if you want to go deeper, it is time for some praise breaks in your life. Life is full of warfare, and praise is your weapon. The Bible is your sword; praise is how you swing that sword. Praise brings you to the inner courts of our beautiful God. Praise is not just necessary to win the battle, it is needed to wake up for another day.

Praise will take you where you need to go when you don't know your next step. Praise will guide you back to God's heart even when you're hurt. When you praise, the Holy Spirit has access to guide your life.

I remember when God told me to make a big move in my life. I was moving from California to Louisiana. Because of the distance, I had no idea how to get there. So I turned on my trusty GPS. A woman's voice began telling me where and when to turn. I hit one highway and the GPS lady said, "Drive for 672 miles." I obeyed the lady and set out on this long highway. After a while I wondered why she was not talking to me anymore. I checked my GPS and it was indeed still working. That's when I realized why she had stopped talking to me: I was still doing the last thing she had told me to do. I had not made this GPS lady upset; she simply had nothing new to tell me. With God, sometimes we have to realize he is silent because he wants us to walk in obedience to what he last said and allow nothing to steal our praise.

I know that God is not always like the GPS lady, but this illustration teaches us that just because God is silent does not mean God is distant. When we praise God, we are welcomed into his presence. His presence and his voice are our GPS in life. This is why we must praise, so we can recognize that pulling a U-turn and going back to our past is not where God is guiding.

Even when God is silent, praise. Even if your spiritual GPS constantly says "recalculating," praise. Praise allows you to move from logic to faith. When you praise you are led to the Father's heart. When you are at the Father's heart, you will know exactly where to go. Stop driving forward while looking in your rearview mirrors. Those exist to help us avoid wrecks, not lead us to our destination.

Praise is the best decision you can make in the midst of trials, stress, or confusion. In fact, I would say that worship is the best decision you can make at any time, in any season and moment of life. Have you ever noticed how the enemy tries to steal your praise through distraction? The moment you engage in worship, your mind starts running through all of the things you need to get done. At least that's what happens to me! The moment I engage God, the devil works overtime to limit my experience. There is a reason the enemy hates it when you worship.

We forget that Satan (Lucifer) was a worship leader. And not just any worship leader. The prophet Ezekiel describes him as "the anointed cherub" and says, "The workmanship of your timbrels and pipes was prepared for you on the day you were created" (Ezek. 28:13–14 NKJV). We can conclude that Lucifer was a high-ranking angel who was once the worship leader for all of heaven, handpicked to lead the angels in chorus. Talk about an incredible job! He was an expert at his craft. He knew how to flow, he knew exactly what song to go to next. He was at the pinnacle of his ministry career.

Nonetheless, Lucifer became prideful. For whatever reason, he allowed pride to seep into the depths of his heart, and he was no longer useful in the heavenlies because of this sin. As a result, God removed Lucifer not just from leading worship but from heaven completely.

So if Satan knows anything (besides sin and lying and being an accuser), it is how to lead worship. As we know, he does not lead any kind of worship that would glorify Jesus. That's not his flow anymore. Now his goal is to prevent God's creation from worshipping the Creator.

Worship is what you focus on more than anything else. Whatever you focus on, you tend to run in that direction. It is not a matter of *if* you worship but *what* you worship. Everyone on this planet worships something, so we must be careful of what or who gets our full attention and adoration.

The devil hates it when you worship. He knows the spiritual impact it will make on your life. I'm sure he remembers that time spent glorifying God in heaven, and even though he loathes it now, it's still a part of his story. The devil is clearly not going to worship God, and he will try to keep you from the power of praise. Satan is out to steal, kill, and destroy the connection you have with Christ when you worship. He hates your worship of God because it reminds him of the glory in which he used to dwell. It reminds him of what he used to be able to do. So whenever the devil reminds you of your past, just remember—your worship reminds him of his.

When you are loved, praise is your pleasure. You know that you have been given a love from God that cannot come from anyone else. As a result, give God your best, most passionate praise every time you get a chance. Thank him for the good and the bad. Thank him in every season. Thank him that his love will endure forever in your life.

In our love story, Gomer had gone missing. Her past had become her present. Hosea contemplated his next move. Should he go find his wife? I'm sure he must have thought, "She's the one who took up prostitution again. Why should I go searching for someone who willingly left me?"

What happens next is scandalous.

STILL

Life is too short, the world is too big, and God's love is too great to live ordinary.

Christine Caine

Then the LORD said to me, "Go and love your wife again, even though she commits adultery with another lover. This will illustrate that the LORD *still* loves Israel, even though the people have turned to other gods and love to worship them."

Hosea 3:1 NLT, emphasis added

You cannot live loved and be lazy. To be lazy would mean you have not fully grasped what the love of God is all about. I mean, you can choose to have a lazy life and still be a Christian. However, real love brings boldness and courage. You no longer fear rejection or failure, because you know even if you fail by the world's standards, you cannot lose the most valuable asset in your life: the love of Jesus.

Real love pushes you away from a cycle of sin. Authentic love encourages you not to sit on your calling. Perfect love casts out all fear because the love of God will cause you to leave all that is comfortable. Isn't that why God sent Jesus? God did the most uncomfortable thing he could have done by sending his Son on a death mission to save humankind. There is nothing lazy or cozy about losing your own son to the world that turned its back on you. God sent Jesus because of love. As John 3:16 says, God so loved this world that he sent his only Son.

God loved us so much that it caused him to make a move that would change the trajectory of humanity. Like an arrow shot, the human soul was headed toward a target of hopelessness. Sin was rampant. Hopelessness at every turn. Something had to change. Someone had to make a move. It was not hope that moved God's heart. It was not a desire for his creations to worship him that prompted him to send Jesus. It was love. Pure, passionate love. A type of love that humans had never experienced and that would redeem any heart willing to accept it. Love is what moved the heart of God.

God's people had terrible standards. They did not earn an ounce of this redemptive love. If God sent Jesus out of a love that was not earned, what makes you think that you have to earn his love today? Love went into action even when we were in corruption. If there was nothing you did to cause God to start loving you, there is nothing you can do to stop his love for you.

Hosea lost his wife to her past. She ran off and was unfaithful to the covenant she made. Then God told Hosea what to do. God did not tell Hosea to let her go. To be honest, that's what Gomer deserved because she was the one who decided to leave. Hosea had every reason in the world to let her have what was coming to her. But God stepped in and the first word he said was, "Go." This word is packed with movement. God told Hosea not to consider all the reasons why he should let her go. Instead, God told him to move out of his logical comfort zone to find the very person who broke his heart.

Oftentimes when we are in a place of struggle or trial, God tells us to keep moving. If you are going through a trial, you cannot afford to stop and look around. In Hosea's toughest moment, God told him to go. God did not tell him to wait. God did not tell him to think about it. God did not tell him to ignore it and things would eventually get better. Nope. God desired movement from Hosea even in the midst of the greatest pain of his life.

The longer I live, the more I realize that life is about going all in. There is no way around it. Our dreams wait on the other side of our full commitment. Is it sometimes scary to go without knowing where God is taking you? Absolutely. However, this is how God builds our trust. As we begin to walk, we learn that he will never leave or forsake us.

You cannot learn that God does not leave you until you are going somewhere. And how do we learn that God will never forsake us? This happens when we understand that with every call of God and every dream in our hearts, there are risks. There will be mountain highs and valley lows. There are faith-building challenges all through this life. Nevertheless, when we are in the midst of a circumstance that could damage our lives, we learn that we are not forsaken. I am not saying that damage will not take place or that all challenges will just go away. I am telling you that, despite the damage that may have happened, God speaks to our hearts to get up and go again.

With both feet, jump off the ledge of safe faith and watch your life be found consistently and constantly in the midst of God's will. There are some things we cannot learn about God until we go. The first two letters of the name God spells "go," right? If we stay where we are, we will get what we have always gotten. Your best life is not the safe life. Your best life is not life on the sidelines. Your best life is facing the giant, climbing that mountain, and going all in on a God who went all out for you.

Then God clarified his command for Hosea to go. God told Hosea to go and love his wife again. Are you kidding me! Couldn't God let Hosea breathe for a minute and collect his emotions? The man just had his heart shattered, and now God was calling him to go rescue the person who shattered it. God told him to go back to the one who created the brokenness and restore that brokenness. God told him to go show love to someone who was unfaithful. This is scandalous. Hosea had done nothing wrong, and God told him to go love the one who did everything wrong. We see some Jesus connections beginning here.

God told Hosea to go and love Gomer again. Hosea had pursued her once before. Now God told him to do it again. It would have been easy for Hosea to ask, Why? He had been loving Gomer and that clearly failed. God will often challenge us to go back and do the very thing we have already been doing, but this time he may bring out a different result.

I am reminded of when Jesus called the disciples away from fishing to follow him. He told Peter to throw his net out into the water again. Peter first replied by telling Jesus he had already tried that. But then he chose to obey anyway. When he did recast his net and did it Jesus's way, he caught an overflow of fish.

God may be challenging you to do something again in your own life. Go to church again, even though you have given up because you have not received what you think you should from church. Go back to your marriage and try again, even though you have tried in the past and feel like it will never work out. With God in your situation, it is always too soon to quit, for he can mend whatever you thought was permanently broken.

Go back to that dream you gave up on and dream again. Go back to your workplace where you feel overused and undervalued and work at a high level again. Go and date again, even though your heart was broken the last time. Go and worship again, even though you feel like you need an answer from God before you can thank him. Truth is, you have plenty of reasons to worship him right now, so go ahead and praise again. Believe again. Hope again. Trust again. Love again. It may be that in the place where you choose to believe again God will decide to do something new.

All of a sudden, this story takes a hard turn. God told Hosea to go and love his wife again even though she had committed adultery. Now, God drops a bomb on us. He says, "This will illustrate that the LORD still loves Israel, even though the people have turned to other gods and love to worship them" (Hosea 3:1 NLT). This is no longer a story about marriage issues or broken trust in a relationship. The story takes a huge turn as God says this is all happening because he has a point to make, and he will use Hosea and Gomer's marriage to reveal that message. This is the purpose of humanity, that we would allow God to make his ultimate point to the world through our lives, as long as we stay obedient to him.

Faithless but Not Forsaken

This story has shifted from the story of a man and a woman to God and his people. This story just became personal for each of us. Hosea is not a self-help book of the Bible where we see God trying to get his people to live more appropriately. Yes, he desires righteousness from his people, but he uses Hosea and Gomer to paint a portrait of a love that the world had never known.

What Hosea did represented how God loved his people Israel, and it also illustrates how God *still* loves his people today. "Still" is the glue to this entire sentence. For one thing, God has no reason to still love his people after the many times they have turned their collective back on him. Why does God still love them? He needs no reason. His love is unreasonable. It does not make sense to the human brain and does not fit into the box of human emotion.

The word *still* means "always; ever; continually." So now let's read Hosea 3:1 while substituting this definition: "This will illustrate that the LORD always, ever, and continually loves Israel." Wow. This is not some cute love we are talking about. This is a love that has endured generations of neglect yet does not cease in its pursuit of the human heart.

This is a game changer. Yes, Jesus loves you. But let's take it one step further: Jesus *still* loves you. This truth is often

tougher to believe than anything else. We think we know that
Jesus loves us, but sin always challenges that truth. Once you
sin, you can learn a lot about yourself. Now, I do not encourage you to keep sinning, thinking that is a good method to
gain more knowledge about who you are. What I am saying
is that you can learn a whole lot about yourself the moment
you fall into sin.

When you sin, what is the first thing you do? What feeling
comes over you? Maybe you have gone so long in sin that you
have become numb to conviction. Conviction is not the shame
game. Many times when people feel the conviction of the Holy
Spirit, they think it is condemnation, as if God is disappointed
with them. This is a lie from the pit of hell. There is no condemnation in Christ Jesus, as Paul says in Romans 8:1. Conviction
is the Holy Spirit leading you back to the heart of God, not
the harm of guilt.

We sin. We feel bad. We try harder. We do better.

We sin again. We feel worse. We try even harder. We do a
little better.

We sin again. We don't know what to do with ourselves. We
want to give up. We remember the pleasure of sin, so we do
that again. We get stuck in the sin cycle.

You've been there, right? No, don't lie to yourself, because
you may be internalizing this book and judging yourself by your
intentions and not your actions. We have all been there. It is
just a matter of how stuck you are on this hopeless carousel of
sin. We all have fallen short of the glory of God (Rom. 3:23).
Now we must learn how to navigate out of this empty pit of
sinfulness in which we find ourselves.

Shame, guilt, and condemnation are not of God. God did not give you any of those feelings. This is why we have to be so careful not to confuse condemnation and conviction. One brings guilt and shame, while the other brings freedom from chains.

So often the first thing we feel after we sin is condemnation. This condemning feeling drags us in the opposite direction of a loving God as we become overwhelmed by guilt and shame. Conviction, on the other hand, is the Spirit of God reminding you that sin is not who you are and that there is a better way for you to live. The Bible describes this as godly grief versus worldly grief:

> For godly grief produces a repentance that leads to salvation without regret, whereas worldly grief produces death. (2 Cor. 7:10 ESV)

Understanding this distinction directly impacts how we receive and think about the love of God. This verse tells us there is a sorrow that God authored. What a strange thought, right? We do not picture God as the author of something like sorrow or grief. However, sin grieves God's heart. It saddens God when we sin. That does not mean he turns his back on us. That does not mean God leaves us high and dry because of this grief he feels. This verse reminds us to be grieved by the things God is grieved by. This is how our relationship with him strengthens and we begin to learn God's heart for our lives. Care about what God cares about and watch your relationship with him strengthen all the more.

But what is the grief God feels? It is sadness that we did not choose him in the moment. Thus, conviction enters the picture to help us build boundaries around our lives. Boundaries and restrictions are not God's rejection but his protection.

I have two very young boys—Braylon, who is one year old, and Beckham, who is almost three. They are the sweetest boys in the world. Sometimes. Beckham has more energy than we know what to do with. If we let him, this little boy will play until he drops. Whenever we go into the front yard to play, he loves to push the boundaries. It is like he gets enjoyment out of torturing his parents in this way. He will go to where he is not supposed to be, then turn around and look at us to see what we are going to do about it.

One of these areas is the street. He will go right up next to the street and turn around to see what we think. When Beckham was younger, we would run and grab him before he could leave the sidewalk; we had to teach him why the street was not a good place to play. We did that over and over again. Eventually, he began to understand that he could not leave the sidewalk without Mom or Dad. We still stuck close to him because you never know with kids, right? Now Beckham knows that the street is not where we play. But there are times when he will still sprint right up to the edge of the sidewalk, turn around, and smile because he knows it freaks us out.

If you are a parent, you totally agree with me that a young child should not be running in the street. We understand the danger of cars, but for the most part our children do not. My son does not know the consequences of playing in the street, and I want to teach him. So I give him boundaries. You wouldn't say these restrictions are harsh or that I am trying to cripple his freedom, would you? Not at all, because I am protecting him from what he does not even see coming.

This is why you cannot reject the restrictions and boundaries God builds in your life through conviction from the Holy Spirit. God protects you from what you don't even see coming. This attitude requires a perspective change. Sin may feel good, but it does not fulfill your soul. It grieves and saddens the heart of God whenever you choose to take on consequences you did not have to experience. And every sin does have a consequence. Yet God's grace for our lives is so much better than the temporary pleasure of our sinful natures.

Godly grief produces repentance. I believe in the power of repentance. You can repent because God has not stopped loving you. You can repent when you feel this godly grief because Jesus absolutely does still love you. Salvation is the result of responding to God appropriately. However, there is a much different ending when we respond to our worldly grief, and it is not happily ever after.

Worldly grief is sorrow that comes from anything of this world. Whether you lose something or you get into a bad situation, you feel a level of depression from this grief. You don't get the job. The divorce goes through. The rumor is true. You lose friends. Trust is broken. You experience financial stress. Something happens that you wish never would have happened. We almost always feel condemnation in such moments, as much as if we had failed spiritually. What happens here is that the world is beginning to tell you how to live, how to think, what you don't have, what you should have, and where you should be by now. Then this grief overcomes you. This sorrow leads you into a sinful cycle where you cannot find hope no matter where you turn. Because this is worldly grief, we think that we will find our healing when the situation improves. However, there is no hope in finding momentary relief from worldly grief. Momentary, situational hope cannot give you what you need in life.

Both godly and worldly grief challenge our ability to live loved. God's grief can be misinterpreted and turned into condemnation instead of conviction. Worldly grief can cause us to continually run to the wrong places to seek the wrong things that will never bring sustaining satisfaction. If we can define these moments of grief, suffering, and difficulty, we will be able to understand Romans 8:38–39, where Paul declares that nothing will ever be able to separate us from the love of God:

> And I am convinced that nothing can ever separate us from God's love. Neither death nor life, neither angels nor demons, neither our fears for today nor our worries about tomorrow— not even the powers of hell can separate us from God's love. No power in the sky above or in the earth below—indeed, nothing in all creation will ever be able to separate us from the love of God that is revealed in Christ Jesus our Lord. (NLT)

If nothing can separate us from this love, then why don't we feel this love as often as we would like? We can feel separated even while reading these verses. It is all in how you define your moments. God's conviction is not separation. Worldly disappointments are not separations. Just because you feel separated does not mean you are. Your disappointments do not distance you from God's love; they cause you to forget where it is and how to access it.

God's love will never leave you, but you can continually walk without acknowledging it. We become our own boundary makers. There are times and spaces where we think we can feel God's love more, leading us to believe that God loves us more in those moments. This is how we end up wrongly evaluating our lives. If we have a good, low-sin day, we feel God's love more since our brain reasons that God is more present because we did better. However, if we have an awful day, or week, or month, then we buy into the notion that God's sorrow means God withholds his love from us.

God's love is not a carnival game where you only get the prize when you win. God's love is not there for you more when you are winning and less when you are sinning. God loves you the same at all times.

Please, please, please see that God has not stopped loving you. The truth that God still loves you can change your world. Whatever you did last night, he still loves you. Whatever line you've crossed, he still loves you. Whatever sin you committed, he still loves you. He still loves you. And guess what? Right now, he still loves you.

He still loves you even though you may be premeditating your next sin. You may know God loves you, but you have not let his love change the way you live. So you sit here reading this book while knowing you are going to keep doing what you are doing and continually break God's heart. You feel trapped and lonely and hopeless. You have written off God's love as the remedy because you think you have the answer and still haven't changed your ways.

Friend, please listen. Do not give God's love only a passing chance. Give God's love everything you've got. You do not need to go back to emptiness any longer. His love will change you in a way you never thought. His love will set the boundaries for your soul. His love will be the satisfaction that is so elusive.

Even when you are faithless, God will not forsake you. When you are unlovable, God still loves you.

DON'T TAKE
THE BAIT

It's time to get healed. It's time to confess. Falling for the bait doesn't make you the worst person in the world. You were snared. You were hooked. But you don't have to stay that way.

Craig Groeschel

I am not a fisherman, but I know many people who love to fish. Not long ago, I made the mistake of asking a fisherman about fishing. I call it a mistake because typically when this happens, you receive a full sermon on fishing. In this case, however, I asked about bait and how to lure in a fish close enough for it to take the bait, thus getting hooked.

His answer was simple and mostly what I figured: "There are certain baits that attract certain fish." Now, I know this is not groundbreaking information. I will also spare you the detailed conversation that followed. But this simple statement about choosing the right bait stuck with me. I could not shake the thought that certain baits target certain types of fish.

Every single one of us has a weakness. You know what I'm talking about here—the one treat that, when you see it, you argue with yourself to stay away. My weakness is sour candy. I struggle in gas stations because there are so many options to fuel my weakness. I get a case of the "I can't help its" and indulge in the nectar that is sour candy. Don't judge me—you know you have a weakness too. My wife's is dark chocolate.

On a deeper note, we all have fleshly weaknesses that are stronger than our desire for sugar. We call them temptations. Temptations never just dissipate and disappear the longer you live. As long as we have breath, we will be tempted. Your spiritual maturity determines how disciplined you are when temptation comes your way. Temptation is a type of bait.

The devil is not omnipresent. He cannot be everywhere at once. That ability is God's alone. Satan is a fallen angel and does not have the power or capabilities of God, but that doesn't mean he is inoperative. He is cunning in his ways and gifted in lying. This is why Satan chooses his timing and battles carefully. You may have experienced this. You are not tempted twenty-four hours a day, seven days a week. You are tempted in moments and spaces where you often did not see it coming. Even if you did see it coming, the devil will attack that area until he sees there is a change in your decision-making.

The devil knows what bait will tempt us. Like a fisherman, Satan casts out bait to people at different times, hoping we'll take it. And just like fish, we think the bait looks good. The bait seems harmless. The bait appears out of nowhere and seems like a great option to take.

However, behind every bait is a hook. This is where the devil gets us. He makes sin look desirable even when we know what it will lead to. He puts that lustful connection right in front of you, and this new bait offers pleasures unknown. Or he places an opportunity in front of you that may seem good, but you know it's not from God. So you battle internally: "Did God really tell me I could not have that / go there / take that?" Isn't that the very way sin entered the world? When the serpent went to Eve, he did not offer sin, he offered doubt. The serpent asked, "Did God really say . . . ?" (see Gen. 3). He will place the bait of your weakness right there for the taking.

What is your bait? If you can define it, you can fight it. You will stay in trouble as long as you ignore those areas in which you know you are tempted. You cannot kill what you will not confront.

What is one temptation you face, something no one else knows about but that you believe will bring about what you desire? Now ask yourself, "Is this bait really going to bring me breakthrough? If I take this, will it bring me into the perfect will of God or out of it?" For example, if you can define your bait as security because you are bound to insecurity, then you can formulate an attack plan.

Are you ashamed of your weakness? Why? Why be afraid of something every person on this planet has? We all have struggles and battles, and we cannot afford to hide them for the sake of appearance. What if I told you that it's in your weakness that God does some pretty amazing things? Life is not about wearing your strength on your sleeve, so no one can actually see who you are. In fact, God is into using your weakness.

But he said to me, "My grace is sufficient for you, for my power is made perfect in weakness." Therefore I will boast all the more gladly about my weaknesses, so that Christ's power may rest on me. That is why, for Christ's sake, I delight in weaknesses, in insults, in hardships, in persecutions, in difficulties. For when I am weak, then I am strong. (2 Cor. 12:9–11 NIV)

You can identify your real weakness by identifying what bait is offered to you the most. If we can be honest with ourselves, we will see that we often cover our real weakness for our "not so bad" weakness. You know, that weakness you don't mind people knowing about. For example, you don't want people to know how strong your battle with depression is, so you hide that by admitting you "get a little discouraged" sometimes. This waters down the real issue. It is a smoke screen that hides the root of the problem. Or you don't want to bring your lust problem into the light, so you hide that issue behind an admission like, "I need to take hold of my mind better." We often flaunt the easier problem to avoid the deeper issue. In fact, it makes us feel a slight relief to admit the lesser of the weaknesses because then people may never find out the real bait we keep taking. But who cares what people see? God sees. That should be enough to make us tired of the secret sickness we put up with and become desperate for spiritual health.

In the 2 Corinthians passage I quoted above, Paul makes a powerful declaration. He doesn't brag about his strengths. He doesn't parade his gifting. He doesn't point out his potential. Not at all. What Paul does is supremely sobering: he unveils what God revealed to him about grace. The grace of Jesus is sufficient. In other words, God's grace is adequate, satisfactory, enough, plenty, appropriate, and necessary. God's grace cannot be optional if you desire a victorious life. For whatever bait the enemy offers, there is grace that is sufficient for you in that moment.

And then Paul hears a ground-shaking statement from God on how God's "power is made perfect in weakness." This is a complete paradox. This does not make full sense to the logical thinkers out there. Why would God choose our weakness to be the platform for his work? Does he not know how hard we try to cover up that part of ourselves? Yet, the thing you try hard to keep from God is what he will turn around and use for your good. The reason God's power may not be working in your life is because you are doing everything in your power to keep your weakness from being seen. Yes, God wants to use what you suck at. There, I said it like I felt it.

Do you struggle with depression? God wants to bring you out of that so you can bring others real joy.

Do you struggle with anxiety? God wants to break this chain so you can be a conduit of his power that releases real peace to people.

Do you battle with lust? God wants you free so people can see that there is a real love waiting to overwhelm them.

Do you battle with offense? It is time to lay that down so God can reveal his healing unity through you.

Do you deal with addictions of any kind? God wants you free of this bondage so you can show people the most addicting thing in life is God's presence.

God's power works best in your weakness. Just let that sink in. The thing you are using to disqualify yourself is the exact thing God wants to turn around and use to reveal his great power. This is amazing! What a deal we get!

So in order to be qualified for this power that God is talking about, we just have to present our weakness to him. Sounds easy, right? This is why the devil tells us that our weakness defines us. In reality, our weakness in the hands of God develops us.

Then Paul continues with elation at the news he just received. His weakness will not kill him, so he's pumped about it. Instead of hiding his weakness, now he is going to boast about it. He is going to claim this weakness as his. It is time to stop letting your weakness go around unclaimed on the baggage carousel of life. Instead, claim it as yours. God won't do anything with unclaimed weakness, but in your weakness God wants to unveil his power.

God is ready to turn your disadvantage into your advantage.

The devious thing about bait, however, is that it hides something beneath the pleasures. Just ask a fish. The next time a fish is caught, go ask it how good the bait tastes. The bait hides a hook. The moment we take the devil's bait, we find it is more than bait.

The devil is not trying to get you to sin once; he wants you bound for life. The bait you take the most is the hook stuck in your life. The devil is OK with your attempts at fixing yourself as long as you don't get to the root of the problem. The enemy becomes your greatest cheerleader when you play the game of excuses. Like how we just talked about hiding our real weaknesses behind lesser ones. The enemy would love for you to be so caught up in the petty issues and hardships and downfalls of your life that you never deal with the root of the stronghold.

Is it possible we have bought into a form of freedom that we have personally defined? A freedom that says, "I'm good as long as I ask God for forgiveness." Or even something like, "I felt God's presence at church, so I'm good now!" I am concerned we are taking the bait of fake freedom. Real freedom is a change of ways, a breakaway from the old, a renovation of your disciplines, a washing of your heart and mind. God wants to forgive your sins and set you free. However, you have to be OK admitting you're not OK. And you have to be OK with the process of freedom that God will walk through with you.

This is why it is so dangerous to think God's grace is just something that will cover me when I am wrong. Friend, grace is so much more. Grace releases the hook in your life and exposes it so you do not keep taking the bait.

The bait looks like pleasure. The bait seems like a good idea. The bait looks like instant satisfaction. The bait may be your numbing mechanism. The bait will always carry more than momentary pleasure. The devil's bait will hook you.

Some of us no longer have a bait problem but a hook problem. We may have taken the bait so often that we are hooked. And we feel guilty when we continue to do what got us hooked, but we cannot seem to stop. We may feel that we cannot help it. It may be too difficult to run from it at this point because the hook has attached to our soul.

So what do we do now? Where do we go from here when the hook seemingly won't let go?

This is where the love of God can overhaul your life.

Love Has a Motive

> There is no fear in love, but perfect love casts out fear. For fear has to do with punishment, and whoever fears has not been perfected in love. (1 John 4:18 ESV)

I have always pictured love, especially Jesus's kind of love, as sensitive and caring. A love that is comforting and peaceful and will never leave. God's love is all that. However, that's not the full story. This love is not just a passive love that allows you to continue in sinful living.

God's love does not equal God's approval. God loves the whole world. Every sinner and every saint. Every person walking in righteousness and those who want nothing to do with Christ. Jesus died for all of humanity, not just those who would love him back. What a shallow love it would be if it was based on our response instead of our existence. We do not deserve love like this, yet Jesus deemed us worth dying for. And not because we were worthy but because he is supremely loving. Because Jesus gave his life for everyone, his love extends to everyone. What a difficult thought. Jesus gave his life for those who despise him and will never turn to him. Yet this is real love.

Jesus died for everyone. Jesus loves everyone. His love level is not based on the character of the person. His love is the same. He cannot help but love every human with this immense love. However, just because he loves everyone does not mean he accepts everyone. This love is meant to bring people in just as they are. But the real love of Christ, once encountered and experienced, will alter the very existence of a life that collides with him. God's love is way more than cute. God's love is so much greater than a feeling. God's love will transform the world you know. God's love has a motive, and that is to kick some things out of your life that cannot coexist with perfect love.

Wait a minute, God's love cannot coexist with my current lifestyle? Is that not contradictory to what love is all about? This is where we have gone wrong. Love is not an approval to continue living a sinful life. Love is the power that possesses you to change everything. Love, real love, has no dark roommates. God's love knows karate and will kick out all that does not belong. Love is not a stamp of approval but a fire that consumes.

This is why God told Hosea to go after Gomer. Love cannot sit still while injustice takes place. Love keeps no record of wrong, which is why Hosea did not hesitate to chase his unfaithful spouse. There was a bigger plan. Love can turn it around. Love can change everything it touches. Even though Gomer ran off, Hosea ran after her. When you run off, the love of Jesus runs after you—not to approve of your lifestyle but to remove you from that lifestyle.

The first part of 1 John 4:18 pits fear versus love, as if love and fear entered the octagon to fight to the death. As though love and fear were archenemies in some superhero movie. The blow to fear comes with the statement "perfect love casts out fear." Here we begin to see the qualities of love even more. Love fights.

For so long I read the word "perfect" and thought it referred to flawless love. However, the original meaning implies something else. Yes, God's love is immaculate and flawless. However, it is not the God-love perfected that casts out fear. God's love is already perfect, so why do we still experience fear? Fear is afraid of the God-love perfected within us. The perfect love of

God is something so much more than our surface level acceptance of it. God's love is to be developed in us.

This is major. Please catch what we just saw in the Word together. To say it is only God's love that casts out fear is to miss the entire point. If you don't recognize this vital difference, you will continue to struggle with fear or whatever else may grip your life. It is not what God possesses that frees you; it is you possessing what God possesses that will break the chains. To simply say, "Because Jesus loves me, fear will not be an issue any longer" is to think that God's love is OK with our laziness. His love and our laziness do not go together at all.

This "perfect" love that is relentless, fiery, constant, and fearless is the love that has been developed in the relationship between you and God. The more you develop love in your relationship with God, the more you will realize that you have all authority over everything that is not of God.

Love undeveloped is love unrealized. The love of Christ is not some distant notion that we call upon to be saved. We must wake up daily and desperately pursue this special love of God. His love never leaves us. Even if we make bad decisions, God's love remains with us.

Have you ever played a video game? Any video game, ever? My go-to back in the day was Mario Kart. Was there a better system than Nintendo? I think not.

Most video games have levels. To get to the next level, you have to complete the level you are currently on. Unless you have cheat codes, you cannot skip to the next level just because you want to. The video game does not care if you want to; it cares only that you complete the level.

This is a bit like what 1 John 4:18 is saying. There are people on different levels with God. This is why comparison is so dangerous—you never know what level or season someone is in or trying to get out of. Just because someone is on level 10, that does not make them better than the person on level 3. It only makes them more developed because they have already been where the level 3 person is. They have grown.

I am not saying God has different levels of his love toward us depending on our individual progress and status. God's love is the same for all of us. I am saying that if you are in level 7, you will only understand a level 7 relationship with God's love. God's love for you has not grown; you have grown deeper in God's love. As each season passes, you start to see that with this love you can make it through anything you face. Your faith grows. Your hope is enhanced. Your foundation in Christ is unshakable as you begin to go from level to level, from glory to glory. There is no ideal level to achieve; the goal should be to keep moving forward.

The longer you live, the more you realize that God's love is evident in places you never thought it could be. It is not because you were ignorant in level 2; you were just way more developed in level 14. Our job is not to define which level we are on but to continue progressing and maturing in the relationship we have with God. As that relationship grows, so does our awareness of God's thoughts and plans.

I had the hardest time understanding love when I was sixteen years old. I was hormonal. I was lustful. I was immature. I was thirsty, if you know what I mean. Sixteen was an interesting year. And if you are sixteen and reading this, I am praying for you.

My teen years were filled with so many unknowns and so much searching. I did not know who I was, so I did what I felt was right to find out what was real. I definitely was not impacted by the thought that Jesus loved me. Between church and the Christian school I was attending, I had heard it thousands of times. However, it never became more than a concept to me. I had not developed in my relationship with God, which led to a lack of understanding about what God's love is and what it could do in me. I believed in Jesus. I would have made it to heaven since he was my Savior. However, this thought of being loved was lost on me.

The strength of your relationship with Jesus is directly proportional to the strength of God's love alive in you. Now that I'm in my thirties and at a different level with God than in my teens, love carries so much more weight. God's love is now the central focus of my life. My focus used to be trying to fill the void in my heart with whatever was in front of me, but God's love is meant to be matured in our hearts.

If you are young and reading this, catch this truth of love now; it will change everything for the rest of your life.

If you are older and reading this, grasp real love now; it will absolutely change every fiber of your being.

Develop and pursue this love as you walk daily with the greatest love to ever exist—the love of Jesus. One of the best ways to begin or reignite your pursuit of God's love is giving him time in your day. Oftentimes we want God to just bust through into our schedule. The reality is that we have scheduled God right out of our day, yet we want him to still be around us. I want to encourage you to wake up earlier if you have to and spend time in prayer with him. Set out moments to read the beautiful and powerful Word God has given us. Keep your thoughts and eyes fixed on Jesus in your coming and going. When you're parenting crazy kids and they've been yelling all day, like I have experienced many times, your mind can still be set on Jesus, and the love of God now has space to enter the moment. It is all about giving God space.

How can God enter your situation if he's never been invited? Take time. Set aside the distractions. Maybe even right now, take a second and thank God, and watch his love lavish over you. Give God space and real love will always be present.

This matured, perfected, developed love makes hell cringe. The presence of strengthened love kicks out fear. You cannot go to the gym once and get a six-pack. Trust me, I have tried. You cannot walk with God once and know you are loved. You have to keep going, keep walking, and keep pursuing the heart of God. It is time to develop the discipline of choosing love so that fear no longer controls you. God's love, alive in the believer, is an unstoppable force.

Love Loves Breaking Up

Love is good at breaking things up. I am not talking about your typical breakup of relationships. I am talking about how this fierce love breaks up the sin party. It breaks up the bondage party. It destroys the enemy's party. Love is a force that nothing can reckon with.

> Love never gives up.
> Love cares more for others than for self.

Love doesn't want what it doesn't have.
Love doesn't strut,
Doesn't have a swelled head,
Doesn't force itself on others,
Isn't always "me first,"
Doesn't fly off the handle,
Doesn't keep score of the sins of others,
Doesn't revel when others grovel,
Takes pleasure in the flowering of truth,
Puts up with anything,
Trusts God always,
Always looks for the best,
Never looks back,
But keeps going to the end. (1 Cor. 13:4–7)

Let's explore each of those statements in more detail.

Love never gives up. Love breaks up with quitting. You cannot simultaneously live in God's powerful love and have the fear of failure in you. It is time to break up with giving up. That means you are done giving up on yourself and giving up on others. Love abounding in you will always believe in you. Listen to the voice of real love that tells you to get back up and try again. Listen to the voice of love as it tells you God is not done with your life yet. Love does not know how to quit. Love never gives up.

Love cares more for others than for self. Love breaks up with selfishness. Love cannot stand thinking about self. Love points outward and forcefully runs to the aid of others. This is Hosea and Gomer. Hosea had every reason to leave her; instead, he decided that real love destroys pride and selfishness. So he went and got his wife back. Love is the end of pride.

Love doesn't want what it doesn't have. Love has broken up with comparison. Love alive in you means no more comparison or lusting after what you do not have. Love is contentment. Love has given an eviction notice to discontentment and lust. Love sees that God has given you all that you need. Love is stronger than envy or jealousy.

Love doesn't strut or have a swelled head. Love points elsewhere. Love can't stand your ego. Love forcefully breaks up with your ego and your need to be seen and noticed. Love does not need a compliment. When you have real love, you won't fight for compliments, because you have a calling. Let love move you beyond your need to be liked.

Love doesn't force itself on others, isn't always "me first." Love is favor. Living in the love of God marks you with a favor unearned. Love is done with you doing things your own way. Love does not need help with your destiny. Love does not need you to force yourself where you do not belong. Love will bring you to the right place at the right time. Love has a pace and a rhythm. Walk to the pace of unforced grace and love.

Love doesn't fly off the handle. Living loved means breaking up with anger. Love and anger cannot be roommates. Anger hates love. Anger will do whatever it takes to suppress love. Where there is anger, there is also lovelessness. Love keeps its cool. Love is slow to speak and quick to forgive. Love is not offended by others. Love keeps you steady and planted. What would our world look like if we simply gave others the benefit of the doubt? Love does that. And love has violently broken up with anger and strife.

Love doesn't keep score of the sins of others. Love means destroying your record of wrongs. I am really good at remembering every bad decision I've made. At least the bigger ones. When love steps in, it serves as a "clear history" to your past searches. Love is done with your remembering what God has already forgiven. God's love does not keep the sin score of others, which means love destroys a judgmental spirit that gossips and brings others down. Love cannot talk that way about others. Love ends conversations that are not compatible with the spirit of God. Love is the greatest encourager, which means with this love living in you, you become a great encourager who will change the atmosphere you walk into rather than conforming to it. Love is done keeping score. Love has so much grace. In fact, if God is love, then love is showing grace to those who don't deserve it. Lead your life giving people the same grace that's already been extended to you.

Love doesn't revel when others grovel. Love does not celebrate at the doorstep of humanity's failure and corruption. Love means breaking up with the spiritual snob inside you. Love does not make you better than everyone, it makes you available to everyone. Love despises bad attitudes toward people. Love does not celebrate others' struggles. Love breeds compassion.

Love takes pleasure in the flowering of truth. Love is breaking up with all lies. God's love detests the lies you believe about yourself. If you allow it, God's love will free you from the personal lies and the enemy's lies you have been listening to. Love exalts truth. Love stands firm in truth even in the midst of a culture filled with corrupt ideologies. Love is what is real in a world full of fake.

Love puts up with anything. I hope my wife is reading this part! Given all that she has had to put up with, I know she loves me. Real love breaks up with conditional love. There are no boundaries on this agape love of Christ. *Agape* is a Greek word used in the New Testament and represents love at its fullest. Agape is not like brotherly love or the love between a husband and wife. It is the most sacrificial, selfless love that exists. It is the word used in John 3:16 when Jesus says, "For God so loved (*agapao*) the world." This love is a covering. Love has patience. Love can wait when it needs to. Love is not overcome by evil, but evil is overwhelmed by love. Love can face anything and stand fearless. Love outlasts our attitudes and resentments. It is time to acquire this patient persistence that is birthed in God's love.

Love trusts God always. Love leans into the heart of God. Love is officially ending your anxiety. Love is done with your way of doing things. Love challenges your faith levels to increase. It is time for you to let love develop a deeper trust for God and his timing. Love is not lonely. You may be alone, but if you have this authentic love, you will overcome loneliness. Love ends your streak of trusting in yourself to get what you want. You must trust God always.

Love always looks for the best. Love obliterates pessimistic thinking and negative living. Love looks. Love sees. Love means you are present in the moment. Love calls you to look for the best in people. Find what is great about people and lift them up. Love searches out greatness. Love will also tell you to do this for yourself. Look for the best in yourself. Encourage yourself if no one else will. Stop waiting for others to approve of you before you move. Jesus has given you everything you need to break through. Lust looks for what it can get. Love looks at what it can give. Lust is out to take. Love is out to give its best.

Love never looks back. Love breaks up with your past. There is nothing in your past that will improve your present. On the positive side, your past can teach you what not to do and where to never go again. Love is future focused. Love compels you to see that you are doing better than you think you are, that you are further along than you realized. Love tells you there is something better ahead of you than what you have come from. Your best days are not over. Your glory days are not behind you. There is so much ahead for you, and nothing can stop God's promise. Love is over being emotional about past relationships, jobs, and concerns. Love will keep you awake. Love cheers you on, shouting, "The best is yet to come!"

Love keeps going to the end. Love is persistent. Love is tenacious. I remember in my football-playing years that one coach described me as tenacious. I had no idea what that meant, so I looked it up. Tenacious means being unwilling to accept defeat or to stop doing or having something. Love makes you live tenaciously. Love will not let you give up the promise God put in your spirit or the dream he gave you. Love will not let you go. Love will not allow you to let go of what you need to keep hold of. Love is a force that causes you to keep going when everything is at its worst. When the world is falling apart, love keeps you intact. Love does not let you live in survival mode, but love encourages you to thrive. Love has no end. Neither should you. Love will not stop. Neither should you.

Now read those verses from 1 Corinthians 13 again, with added commentary to make it personal:

> Love never gives up. (Neither do I.)
> Love cares more for others than for self. (So do I.)
> Love doesn't want what it doesn't have. (Neither do I.)

Love doesn't strut. (Neither do I.)
Love doesn't have a swelled head. (Neither do I.)
Love doesn't force itself on others. (Neither do I.)
Love isn't always "me first." (Neither am I.)
Love doesn't fly off the handle. (Neither do I.)
Love doesn't keep score of the sins of others. (Neither
do I.)
Love doesn't revel when others grovel. (Neither do I.)
Love takes pleasure in the flowering of truth. (So do I.)
Love puts up with anything. (So do I.)
Love trusts God always. (So do I.)
Love always looks for the best. (So do I.)
Love never looks back. (Neither do I.)
Love keeps going to the end. (So do I.)

With love alive in you, these are all real results that can take place in your life if you so choose.

Don't take the bait of fake. God is always a better choice.

HIGHEST BIDDER

Hope is being able to see that there is a light despite all of the darkness.

Desmond Tutu

So I bought her back for fifteen pieces of silver and five bushels of barley and a measure of wine.

Hosea 3:2 NLT

The last we read in this dysfunctional love story was how Hosea, the husband, went to find his wife, Gomer, who had chosen to run off and run around. This is a soap opera of Bible stories if I have ever read one. Juicy. Filled with plot twists. Overwhelming on the emotions. But God is about to use this crazy story to reveal something that will change everything.

After Hosea heard God's command to go after his wife again, he went searching. He left the kids with a sitter and went where no man of God should be seen. He went down to the backstreets where his wife was known as a regular. There he was on a dark night, walking in the presence of immorality. What if someone recognized him and assumed the worst? What if someone posted on social media that your pastor was spotted hanging around your city's red-light district? This was not the best place for a prophet of God to be seen. However, this was where God had called him to go.

We must break the notion that being a man or woman of God separates us from a society filled with sin. Hosea was not becoming the culture, he was bringing love to a dark place. Jesus was a friend of sinners. How can we win a world that we are distanced from? We do not embrace immorality to reach people; that is a ridiculous idea. However, we are called to love all people and to be a light in the darkness. It is time to get out of the pews and show Jesus in the streets.

As Hosea walked around those streets, he happened upon an auction in progress. Now, this was not your typical auction. This was a slave auction that sold people to the highest bidder. As he walked in, Hosea looked desperately for his wife. The auctioneer must have said something like, "Next up we have a local favorite, Gomer. She left everything to be here tonight, so let's start the bidding."

I can see Hosea rushing over to the auctioneer, pleading with him to take Gomer off the block because she is his wife. The man probably told Hosea, "I can't do anything about it. She walked in here. We are going to sell her to the highest bidder."

Hosea desperately replied, "No, but you don't understand. That is my wife. She belongs to me. Just let her come home with me!"

The owner looked back and said, "Look, sir, I do not care who she is to you. If you want her back, you will have to buy her back. Those are the rules. She goes to the highest bidder; end of discussion."

Once again Hosea had a decision to make. He could allow her to get what was coming to her—to be bought by someone who would abuse her. Or he could buy back what already belonged to him.

The sale of Gomer began, and bids started coming in. One bidder was about to win her. "Going once. Going twice," the auctioneer yelled.

"Wait!" Hosea replied. "I'll buy her for fifteen pieces of silver and five bushels of barley and a measure of wine." The place went silent. Everyone looked at each other, not understanding what just happened or who this mystery man was.

"Going once. Going twice. Sold! To the man in the back who just walked in. Come up and claim your prize."

That is how this part of the story played out in my mind. What an unpredictable twist of events. However, this moment is drenched in significance and revelation that we will miss if we move ahead too quickly.

Hosea was not just bidding to buy back his wife. He was bidding to buy back his unfaithful wife who had broken his heart and might not even be sorry for her actions. Love drove him to that place.

But wouldn't it make more sense for Hosea to wait for a well-deserved apology? From what we are told, Hosea had done nothing wrong. Gomer ran off. Gomer got herself on that auction block. Gomer apparently felt no remorse. Nonetheless,

Gomer's actions did not stop Hosea's pursuit. No matter how hard Gomer made things, real love would overcome.

This is shocking and goes completely against human nature and reason. If we have been wronged, we want an apology before we pursue reconciliation. However, here God teaches us to let nothing stop us from pursuing reconciliation with our brothers and sisters, husbands and wives, and any other relationships that may be divided. God's call to reconciliation is part of his redemptive plan for humankind.

Hosea faced a life-altering decision. I am not sure what ran through his head in that moment, but maybe all he could hear was God telling him to love his wife again because that would demonstrate God's love for his people. So Hosea stepped up and bought back Gomer.

Hosea bought back what was already his. Wait, he did what? He bought back his wife who had broken their marriage covenant? And received no apology? Yes, you are reading this story correctly. And I'm as shocked as you are, even though I have read this story many times. He bought back what was already his. This is a major moment in the story.

Hosea placed the highest bid for someone he had no obligation to buy back. But remember, this story is not just about Hosea and Gomer; it's about God and his people.

This story represents what Jesus did on the cross. He paid the ultimate price to buy back what was already his. As we discussed in previous chapters, we were made in the image of God—his breath in our lungs, his life in our bones. Without God, we would cease to exist. We belong to him because he made us. He is our creator. He is our maker. He is our everything.

When sin entered the world, it caused a chasm between us and God. But God the Father had a better plan. He sent his own precious Son to buy back what already belonged to him. Hosea's story models this long before Jesus was even born.

Like Gomer, we were on an auction block, which means there were other bidders. You better believe death, hell, and the grave were bidding for your soul. Satan was willing to pay a price for you, but he could not get close to matching the ultimate, invaluable price of Jesus Christ.

Hosea illustrates a love no one can fathom, a love that changed the existence of humanity. What kind of love would pay a price to buy something that already belonged to him? Yet Jesus did. On the cross he paid the price for us. He got what we deserved so we could get what we don't deserve. Salvation. Hope. Love that radically alters everything. This is a crazy love.

So when you think you are unloved, think instead about the cross. That was a payment for your life. And why did Jesus do it? Love. He loves you that much.

Love Finds. Love Fixes.

When I was about eleven years old, I loved making up things to do when I got really bored, and on this one particular day, I was beyond bored. I remember walking into the kitchen and doing something pretty strange. I opened a cabinet door and sat on it. I was just tall enough that my tiptoes could touch the ground, so most of my body weight was on the door. As I sat on it, I swung back and forth. No real reason. I was just bored. It's probably safe to say I needed more friends in my life at this age.

My dad came in the kitchen and saw me swinging and immediately told me to get off the door. He said if I kept swinging, I would break it.

I hopped off, even though I did not agree with him. I mean, why would it break? I was super skinny and it was fun. At that moment, I was convinced my dad was out to make my life as unenjoyable as possible.

A few minutes passed and my dad left the kitchen. Well, that door called to my soul. I could not pass up my dreams of swinging. You may say this is pretty lame, but I will challenge that by saying you most likely have never done it. You should go try it. Right now. It's a thrill.

Now that you're back, let me go on with my story. My dad left, so I jumped back on the door and swung back and forth, vaguely remembering his warning that I would break it.

A few minutes in, all was well. Then, out of nowhere, I hit the ground so hard I didn't know what happened to me. I remember looking up at the ceiling with this cabinet door lying on me, and I realized what I had done. This was one of those moments where I believed in prayer. I started praying that God would spare my life, because my dad was going to kill me for breaking the door!

I got up from the crime scene and took a look at the damage. It was bad. It looked like I had ripped the door from its hinges. I thought, *There's no way Dad is going to fix this; it's too bad.* So I did the most helpful thing I knew how to do before my dad returned and saw my colossal mistake: I ran to my room, shut the door, turned off the lights, sat balled up in the corner, and cried. Yes, this is a true story. And I did not just cry, I bawled my eyes out. I was crying because I knew my dad would eventually find out and then find me.

Time began to pass in that room. Twenty minutes turned into an hour. An hour turned into three hours. Yes, I cried on the floor in my room for three hours over a broken kitchen door. What can I say? I was a sensitive kid. This was not my finest hour.

After three hours of sulking, I finally heard my dad's footsteps walking down the hallway. I had no idea what was going to happen. I was scared out of my mind. But it was time to be a man and face the music.

Dad walked into my room and turned on the lights. He spotted me and looked confused as he asked, "Son, what's going on? Are you OK? Why are you crying?"

I was also confused, since I thought for sure he knew why I was hiding. However, I did my best to answer—although through the hard crying, I could not talk very well. I mumbled that after he told me not to swing on the cabinet door, I did it anyway, and it broke like he said it would.

My dad, beyond puzzled by what I was telling him, looked at me and said, "Son, I fixed that door three hours ago, right after you broke it. I was not worried at all about the door. I was just worried that I had not seen you for the last couple hours."

Wait, he did what? My dad fixed what I broke. Not long after I broke it. He was not concerned about it like I was. And he wanted to find me and make sure I was OK even though I had made the mistake.

Wow. What a picture of what happened to Gomer and of what Jesus does for you and me. When we sin, Jesus fixes it. In fact, he already fixed it on the cross. Whatever you have done, do not sulk about it. Do not run off to your room of guilt and shame and mull over all you have done and how God is going to punish you once he finds you. No, friend! That is not the case with Jesus at all. What he did on the cross one time is strong enough to cover your mistakes every time. He finds you. He fixes you! He does this because he is so very good.

My dad found me in my room of guilt to tell me he had already fixed what I was crying over. Hosea went and bought back what was already his, effectively fixing what Gomer had ruined. Jesus found us by becoming human, walking among us, living a perfect life, dying a sinner's death, taking back the keys of death, hell, and the grave, and rising again after three days. He forever fixed our broken lives with a love that we had never known before. It is up to us to walk in this love.

Friend, there never has been nor will be a better love in the universe than this love from the heart of God. Love has found you. Let love fix you.

Before we move on, let's look at another translation of Hosea 3:2. The New Living Translation I quoted earlier says, "So I bought her back." But if we compare the New King James Version, we see a little twist on the language: "So I bought her for myself." This goes a bit deeper than the NLT and gives insight into Hosea's reasoning for such a powerful moment. He bought Gomer for himself. Indeed, through the character of Hosea, love finds Gomer. But love goes further. Love is in it for keeps. The love of God is not just meant to find you but to keep you in close proximity to the Father's heart.

You were not just bought *by* someone but *for* someone. You were not just saved *by* someone but *for* someone so you can do something. God did not send Jesus so you and I would still belong to the world. Jesus is more than a Christmas and Easter story. The love of God is more than a feel-good notion for the believer looking to be comforted and not challenged. Jesus bought you back at a high price; don't sell yourself cheap. Jesus purchased our lost souls so that we would find a home in him. He did not give up his life so we could spend ours trying to find a fake replacement for real love. He is the real love that we so desperately need, even if we do not know we need it.

Gomer stood on that auction block without hope. She was miserable. Lust, insecurity, and depression led her to a place she never wanted to go back to.

Have you ever been there? Standing on the foundation you built only to feel hopelessness and depression as a result? God had nothing to do with your ending up there. But he has everything to do with your not staying there. You may have gotten yourself in this thing pretty deep, but there is no ditch too deep that the love of God will not be able to find you out and bring you up.

Love is searching for you. Stop looking for fake replacements for God's tangible presence. And once you let love find you, love will fight for you. You can walk away from it, but love will not leave you.

Paid in Full

Hosea 3:2 reveals to us the price Hosea paid to get his wife back. He paid fifteen pieces of silver, five bushels of barley, and a measure of wine. Aren't you grateful we don't pay that way anymore? It would be tough to carry bushels as you walk around the mall.

But let's look closer here. When I first read this story, I paid no attention to the payment amount. I just kept chugging through to the following verses. After reading it through dozens of times, however, I stopped and paid attention to the payment amount. Fifteen pieces of silver and five bushels of barley are the main portion of payment.

It is no secret that numbers in the Bible often carry meaning. Not every number, but there are some numbers that when you study them, you find a deeper understanding of the Word of God. In the case of Hosea's payment, the numbers fifteen and five both happen to be significant Bible numbers.

The number fifteen in the Bible means "rest." The Feast of Unleavened Bread began on the fifteenth day of the first Hebrew month. This was a day of rest for the children of Israel. The Feast of Tabernacles began on the fifteenth day of the seventh month, which was also a day of rest.[3] This rest does not mean physical rest like sleeping well or taking a nap. It is a spiritual overwhelming that refreshes the soul and clears the conscience. Interestingly, the number fourteen represents deliverance. So literally, this is the rest that comes to you once repentance and deliverance from sin take place. It is the type of rest that feels like a burden has been lifted off your shoulders. It is that redemption moment where you know your past is done and Christ has forgiven you. Hosea bought his wife back with fifteen pieces of silver. This symbolizes that Jesus bought us back with redemptive rest. The kind of rest where you have peace beyond understanding. The kind of rest that the devil cannot steal. This is your rest. And this rest is a promise.

This rest does not depend on life going your way. The quality of this rest does not come from your quality of life. Everything in life could be falling apart, but this rest is still a promise at your disposal. This rest reminds you to see life from heaven's perspective, not yours. Rest today. Rest in knowing that God will fight every battle. Rest in knowing that if God spoke it to you, it will come to pass.

Hosea also bought Gomer back with five bushels of barley. The number five is one of the most powerful numbers in the Bible because it represents the grace of God. Five is mentioned 318 times in Scripture. Five times five is "grace upon grace" (John 1:16). The tabernacle in the wilderness reflected God's grace in its use of the number five: it contained five curtains (Exod. 26:3), five bars (26:26–27), five pillars, and five sockets (26:37), and an altar that was five cubits long and five cubits wide (27:1). The height of the court within the tabernacle was five cubits (27:18). The holy anointing oil, used to consecrate the furniture of the tabernacle, had five ingredients, for it was a revelation of pure grace (30:23–25).[4]

Hosea bought back Gomer with five bushels of barley. Jesus also bought us back with his wonderful grace. Grace is getting what we do not deserve. Grace is unmerited and undeserved favor from our God. We did not deserve Jesus, we deserved death. So grace came in human form, Jesus, and took our place and kept us from getting what we ultimately deserved. Grace is so much more than a word, however. Grace is a person. Jesus is grace alive. We have this amazing favor and the opportunity to hand our nasty sins over to a loving God because Grace himself came down. We were bought with grace and by grace.

There is no salvation without grace. We should be waking up daily and thanking our heavenly Father for this unbelievable, undeserved, outrageous grace.

Jesus bought us back, but it was at a price. Here in Hosea, we see that we were bought back with the very things we cannot live without: rest and grace. It is time to live in this rest and grace that have been paid for us.

This is not to shortchange the sacrifice Jesus made. Jesus gave it all and paid it all. However, what Hosea reveals to us is that our freedom is predicated upon our understanding of the power of rest and grace. Living in supernatural rest means you are walking in a peace that only comes from knowing you are free and delivered from every chain. Living in God's grace is not an entitlement to stay bound. Grace not only saves us, it breaks the bondage of the sins that try to grip us.

On the cross Jesus said, "It is finished." Three of the most powerful words in the entire Bible. The word he spoke was *tetelestai*. This word has a crazy powerful meaning. You could write a whole book on the word *tetelestai*. Maybe someday I will. At its heart, the word means "paid in full." Jesus chose to use some of his last words to describe his payment. His last words become our first words. We have life because he gave his. We are loved because he poured out all of his love on us. We can walk boldly in rest and grace because Jesus has paid it all, and paid it in full, for every single one of us.

Live in the love of God like you need nothing more in life. Live in the complete work of Jesus, who fulfilled hundreds of laws and prophecies not so we could start another denomination but so we would follow him. On the cross he said, "It is finished," not "I am finished." He is still working all things together on your behalf. While you are waiting, he is working. While you are sleeping, God is working things out.

Live in wholeness. Live in the finished work. Live in this earthshaking, sin-redeeming love. Live in this supernatural rest and grace. The price has been paid in full.

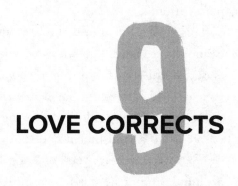

LOVE CORRECTS

You were born looking like your parents. You die looking like your decisions.

Bishop Dale Bronner

For the LORD corrects those he loves, just as a father corrects a child in whom he delights.

Proverbs 3:12 NLT

If God loves you, God will correct you. In fact, God will correct you even if you do not know that he loves you. That is a dangerous place to be, however. When the Holy Spirit nudges us to stop doing something or to run from a decision, we take it as either protection or persecution. When God corrects a person who knows he loves them, they tend to take God's correction as protection. On the other hand, many people do not know or believe that God loves them. Or maybe they think he does but have no clue what that means and why it is relevant to their lives. God will still attempt to correct those people, although they do not fully grasp his love and will see that correction as persecution.

This is why living in real love is vital for the believer. You cannot have a fruitful relationship with Jesus if you believe he is out to kill your fun and punish you at every turn. Maybe you see God as a rule-monger just trying to get his way and make your life more difficult. Or maybe you feel like every correction is a punishment and are overwhelmed by guilt and shame when God says "no" or "stop." You feel this way as an accumulation of how you were raised and what you believe about the love of God.

Nevertheless, Proverbs 3:12 paints a clear picture for us: love corrects. When God corrects you, it is because he loves you. And if you know his gripping love and are firmly planted in it, you will take to heart every word God speaks. He corrects because he cares. He delights in you. He cherishes you. But he really wants to change that sinful you. To get to your calling, you have to listen to correction.

No one likes correction. There is nothing sexy about correction. Correction is the part of Christianity many people want nothing to do with. It is hard to be told something about yourself that needs to change. We all have things we call blind spots. Have you ever tried to talk to a person about their blind spot? It's easier to run in mud than to tell someone they have an issue they don't see. Many of my blind-spot conversations with people end on the rocks because they choose not to believe what I tell them.

People will believe what they want to believe. Those who will not listen to correction are choosing to live in their own reality. We all have flawed perspectives that need to be challenged. So when God or your pastor or a leader wants to discuss some changes in your life, don't take it as punishment. Take it as protection. And if you do change according to what God spoke to you, it will set you up for where God is about to take you.

My son, Braylon Malachi, is so full of energy and life and the sweetest little boy. He is also very inquisitive. One day I caught my little guy reaching up toward the stove. As I watched him, I thought about allowing him to touch it so he could learn that fire and fingers don't go well together. However, the better parent in me came through, and I shouted his name and ran over in time to save him just before he could get burned.

Isn't it interesting that even though parents have been teaching this lesson for many years, children are not born with the understanding that a stove is hot? It's because there are some lessons that need to be taught in order to be caught. And I have to stay consistent with both of my little boys about playing with or around fire. It is a slow process of learning, but it is for their safety. I am not keeping them away to destroy their joy. I am doing it to protect them from dangers they don't even understand.

There are lessons from God that we cannot learn any other way except through correction. When we get stuck in the bubble of our own reality, we think we know what we need to know. But the first step to wisdom is admitting you do not know everything. We were not born with knowledge. We were born into this sinful world with the ability to choose. You cannot control what you were born into, but you can control where you end up.

Being loved by God means more than comfort. Being loved means being enrolled in a process. We often miss this side of accepting real love. The process is to prune us and sharpen us to be better than we once were. I love how C. S. Lewis said, "God will make us good because He loves us."[5] We all want that to happen. We all want to be good people, especially in a culture and time where we need good and godly people to step up like never before and express love, not judgment. This process to becoming a better human is painful. It takes correction. It takes hearing things about yourself you would never want to hear. It takes admitting faults and forgiving offenses.

God does not love you based on how good or bad you are. That's conditional love. The unconditional, agape love of God overrides what you have done and loves you for you. But when you fully receive and become enveloped by this intoxicating love, God will correct you right into your calling.

Sometimes You Need a No to Grow

There is a reason why sheep need a shepherd and are surrounded by fences. There is a reason for speed limit signs on streets. There is a reason we have police officers and firefighters. There is a reason babies ride in car seats. There is a reason why doors have locks. There is a reason many people have home security systems. There is a reason you have to wear a helmet in football. The reason for these restrictions is not to slow everything and everyone down. These restrictions provide protection. Whatever God has said, trust him. He is protecting you from something you may not ever see coming.

Correction hit Hosea's household after he bought back his wife. When Gomer returned, Hosea outlined some critical steps on how she should move forward if she wanted to leave her past behind:

> Then I said to her, "You must live in my house for many days and stop your prostitution. During this time, you will not have sexual relations with anyone, not even with me." (Hosea 3:3 NLT)

Hosea told Gomer that she must live in his house for a season. Her first step of correction involved changing locations. She could not hang out where she used to. She could not have the same friends who would pull her backward. It was time for her to live in a different house. Hosea's house. The name Hosea means "salvation," so for Gomer, it was time to live in salvation's house.

For us this is not so much a physical place as it is a spiritual place. You cannot claim spiritual health yet be sleeping around. You cannot say "God promised me" and see that promise come to life unless you walk in God's ways. You cannot be a Christian in a church service yet look just like the world every other moment outside of that service. The days of falling for what is fake or being a part of what is fake have to end.

Whose house are you really living in? God wants you in his house. And yes, that includes God's church. You cannot be fully in God's perfect will yet be offended and separated from his church. Churches are not perfect, but I promise that some are doing an incredible job of bringing heaven to earth. Go find one and plug into it right away. The first step in God's correction for your life is getting you out of what you have been stuck in. It is time for your surroundings to change. The only way they change is if you make the decision to leave toxic relationships and friendships behind.

Hosea 3:3 reminds us that we must live in God's sweet presence. You must live in God's house. Every moment of every day you have full access to live in the love and presence of Jesus Christ. It is time to change your home address. It is time to move out of compromised living. This is your moment to take your life back and get back to the heart of God.

Next, Hosea told Gomer that she must stop her prostitution. That's an obvious one, right? If you want to stay married, remove the issue that is tearing the marriage apart. In Gomer's case, it's clear that if she does not stop her prostitution, the marriage will not last.

Once we get back to the heart of God, we find there are many things we need to stop doing. Let me ask you, in light of some of the decisions in your life, what in the world are you doing? You're right—I don't know you and I have no context of your journey. But maybe you read my question with the wrong emphasis. I'm not condemning you. Let's read it with a different emphasis: What *in the world* are you doing? What are you doing in your life that Christ has nothing to do with? There are elements of your world that Christ wants to remove. We are living in this world and are hopefully alive in Christ as well. But you cannot simultaneously be of the world and of

Christ. Scripture teaches that we must be in the world but not of it (John 17:16). We no longer belong to this world but have been chosen to come out of it (John 15:19).

Hosea told Gomer to straight-up stop. He placed an immediate halt on her sin life. What is it in your life that you know God is telling you to stop, but you haven't yet? Until you stop, you will be stuck in this season. You can pray for a new season, but maybe entering that new season doesn't depend on your passionate prayer but on your disciplined response to God's command to stop. You will not be able to truly GO for God until you STOP what God is telling you to end.

Hosea didn't just tell Gomer to stop her sin; he told her to stop her performing. He told her to stop faking that she had no issues and everything was OK. He wanted her to be in a new location and not have an old mind-set. And this is also God's call for you and me. There's no more performing once you are in the right house.

Everything outside of God's love is a performance-driven life. You try to keep up yet are failing. You try to acquire things on your own to no avail. You act like a Christian but your faith is seriously shaken. You are depressed, so you perform joyfully for the people at church—as if God were calling you to act perfectly when in fact he calls you to pursue perfection. Once you are out of the house of the world, you need not continue your performance. Some of the greatest actors are not in Hollywood, they are in the church. Quit the Hollywood-level acting when it comes to who you really are. Stop the performing. You have nothing to prove to people. Live for that audience of One. Please the heart of God and your life will align with dreams beyond your comprehension. But to become healthy you must put an end to this charade. No more games. No more secrets. The jig is up. Bring your whole self back to the love of Jesus, and he will restore you from the inside out.

What I particularly love about Hosea 3:3 is that it assures us that God is with us through the entire healing process. He is not saying, "Come back to my house, stop your performing, and I will send you out to the nations tomorrow and use you greatly!" I think Christians are a bit too cause-and-effect minded. We are also impatient. Is that too harsh to say? I apologize, but I totally believe it. We think that God saves us only to send us. God sends us because we have a walking, working relationship with the Savior of the universe. There will be a time for those assignments to happen in your life.

As Christians, we are so task-oriented that we think we are unsuccessful until we do great things. But greatness is not something you do. Greatness is who you are. You do not accidentally arrive at greatness. Greatness has to do with your character and integrity. God wants to give you influence, but he does not want to take you where your character won't keep you. Getting back to God's presence and learning his pace is the best decision you can make.

Spiritual health is not a sexy idea to most people. Influence is sexy. Power is sexy. Financial gain is sexy. However, in the kingdom of God, health has to be our priority. While you are hurrying to get somewhere, slow down. Growth is about becoming someone pure. Life with love is about constantly living in God's presence even though you are surrounded by traps. God will not leave you. God wants to walk with you.

He wants a conversation. Yes, he may correct you within that conversation. That is a good thing. Walk in love and you will never fall for what's fake. When busyness defines your life, slow down, get spiritually healthy, and watch your life improve. Love is correction.

UNMASKED
AND UNDONE

To have found God and still to pursue Him is the soul's paradox of love.

A. W. Tozer

Hosea 3 is a brief chapter, but it tells the whole love story between Hosea and Gomer. The final two verses, however, carry a different tune than the others.

> This shows that Israel will go a long time without a king or prince, and without sacrifices, sacred pillars, priests, or even idols! But afterward the people will return and devote themselves to the Lord their God and to David's descendant, their king. In the last days, they will tremble in awe of the Lord and of his goodness. (Hosea 3:4–5 NLT)

While the previous verses were story-centered, these power-packed verses are prophetic.

When Scripture says "This shows," it reminds us that the story of Hosea and Gomer represents God and his people Israel. This story is meant to be read as symbolic and show us God's real love for humanity.

Israel would go a long time without performing sacrifices or acts for God. However, a time was coming, for the Israelites and for us, when sacrifices would be eliminated by the greatest sacrifice.

This passage turns a corner and becomes intriguing when it speaks of the people of God and their devotion. I love this thought of devotion. I believe devotion to God is everything because it is shown in so many ways. You show your devotion to God by how you live your life, how you run your schedule, whether you trust him in every moment, and how much priority you place on your relationship with him.

God is calling us back to full devotion, the kind that is intimate and vulnerable before the Lord. Not just reading a devotion a day but having a committed relationship with the Lover of our souls. A real devotion that no storm in life can destroy and no devil in hell can steal. An unashamed devotion that you don't just live out in a church building on Sunday morning but that comes alive in you every morning you wake up. If his mercies are new every morning, your pursuit should be passionate every day.

God is calling us back to his heart in these crazy days because it's there we will find true joy and peace beyond understanding. This is not the time to be a weakly devoted Christian. The days of living silently in our faith are over. God's love should compel you to step up and step out in faith. No matter where you live, this is the moment for Christians to get a backbone of steel and begin letting their devotion to God lead the way for their hearts.

Just because you are loved does not mean you live silently. Because you are loved does not mean you stop fighting for those in need, for "the least of these" (Matt. 25:40). Love is like a fire in your bones that will cause you to violently attack the gates and schemes of hell, because your life is not about you anymore. Devotion to God is more important than anything else in this life, and God is calling us back. Back to our first love. Back to the One who gave his life for us even though he knew many would deny him. Back to a devotion that is undeniable.

We can no longer display Bible verses on the walls of our homes if those verses do not seep into the souls living in those homes. God's Word is so much more than a coffee shop Instagram post of your Bible next to a venti triple-shot soy mocha latte. Worship is so much more than a few minutes of songs on Sunday mornings. Prayer is so much more than just blessing your meal and then moving on with your day. Devotional living is not momentary living. Devotional living means God has your heart at all times and is a part of every decision. Yes, your devotion to God will impact your every decision.

When you are fully devoted to this great love of God, insignificant things do not steal your attention or adoration away. Many things in life compete for your focus. And where your focus goes, so does your worship. This is the danger of our time: distraction. We are the most distracted society in history. We lose our attention in seconds and need constant entertainment. However, God is not into entertaining you into a real relationship with him. You cannot let worldly distractions turn you away from spiritual encounters. There is more for you to experience with God. He draws you to intimacy if you open your ears. He loves you, but he wants you to experience this love. There must be a time in your life where you no longer let distraction steal your devotion.

If the devil cannot destroy you, he will distract you. The devil is OK with your going to church as long as he can keep you from becoming the church. But when you devote your life to Christ, you will become all that Christ has called you to be.

We cannot live as masked Christians any longer. We must become unmasked and undone before Christ. The only thing a mask does is hide the identity of the one wearing it. Your calling is not to show people who you are not. There is no need to hide your hurt. It is not necessary for you to fake your friends out by covering up who you really are. For example, if you deal with suicidal thoughts, don't be quiet about that. Speak up and talk to someone who loves you. More importantly, talk to God about your struggle. That is the beauty of devotion: it is not about perfection but pursuit.

Take off the mask. Put away the distractions. Get alone with God. Seek his heart with everything you have. Stop living for the applause of others. And become solely devoted to a loving God who will shock you at what he can do with your life. He wants to know you more, and you should want to know him more than anything else.

If you decide for God, living a life of God-worship, it follows that you don't fuss about what's on the table at mealtimes or whether the clothes in your closet are in fashion. There is far more to your life than the food you put in your stomach, more to your outer appearance than the clothes you hang on your body. Look at the birds, free and unfettered, not tied down to a job description, careless in the care of God. And you count far more to him than birds.

Has anyone by fussing in front of the mirror ever gotten taller by so much as an inch? All this time and money wasted on fashion—do you think it makes that much difference? Instead of looking at the fashions, walk out into the fields and look at the wildflowers. They never primp or shop, but have you ever seen color and design quite like it? The ten best-dressed men and women in the country look shabby alongside them.

If God gives such attention to the appearance of wild-flowers—most of which are never even seen—don't you think he'll attend to you, take pride in you, do his best for you? What I'm trying to do here is to get you to relax, to not be so pre-occupied with *getting,* so you can respond to God's *giving.* People who don't know God and the way he works fuss over these things, but you know both God and how he works. Steep your life in God-reality, God-initiative, God-provisions. Don't worry about missing out. You'll find all your everyday human concerns will be met.

Give your entire attention to what God is doing right now, and don't get worked up about what may or may not happen tomorrow. God will help you deal with whatever hard things come up when the time comes. (Matt. 6:25–34)

Jesus over Everything

I am reminded of the Bible story where Mary poured the alabaster jar of perfume over Jesus (see Matt. 26:6–13; John 12:1–8).

The Mary in this narrative was a follower of Jesus, not the mother of Jesus. Much like Gomer, Mary had a shameful past. She had been possessed by demons and was a prostitute, among other things. No, she had not been living her best life. Then we see her break through the house doors with a jar of perfume and make a beeline for Jesus. This is crazy!

The first thing I notice is that she approached the house where Jesus was and did not wait outside the doors until she felt like she was clean enough or good enough to be around him. Mary came into the presence of Jesus boldly and confidently; she came just as she was, not as she thought she should be.

The people at the table with Jesus were not your normal churchgoing believers. Jesus was eating in the home of Simon, who was freshly healed of leprosy. You have some definite sinners at the table, including Judas Iscariot, who was already plotting to sell out Jesus. The person I find really intriguing is Lazarus. Lazarus had been recently raised from the dead, so he was probably thinking, "How did I even get here? Is this bread gluten-free? I just died; I can't be eating anything and everything anymore." At least that's my best guess of what Lazarus was thinking.

Mary decided that mid-meal and mid-conversation was the perfect time to interrupt Jesus and pour her jar of perfume over him. This perfume was an extravagant gift costing up to a year's wages. Mary was unconcerned with who was looking at her or what they might say about her as she chose to worship in this undone manner. Jesus did not send her away; his love was displayed powerfully toward her and what she had done.

Mary then did something a bit strange. Mary fell at the feet of Jesus, let down her hair, and began to wipe his feet with her hair. I know many people always say, "What a beautiful moment!" I understand the sentiment. However, I am not a big foot person. Nor am I a big hair-on-feet person. So all of this feels awkward for me. But there was indeed so much beauty in that moment.

The climactic moment of this story, I believe, happens between what Mary gave and what she did. Mary gave expensive perfume. We often focus only on the price of this gift, but what about its meaning? Do you remember how Mary had a past? She had been a harlot, a prostitute. Walking the streets each night, she most likely would have picked up an unclean smell. A dirty scent. An odor that resulted from her lifestyle. Perfume, as you know, is used to cover up unpleasant odors. It temporarily masks your real scent. What if Mary did not just see her perfume as an expensive gift but as the very thing that covered up where she had been? Mary gave this perfume because she was done hiding behind this mask. She did not just give God a gift; she gave him her cover-up. No more filters. No more faking. No more hiding.

The other important moment is when Mary let down her hair so she could wipe Jesus's feet in a powerful display of worship. In those days, it was a big deal when a woman let down her hair. A woman's hair represented her glory. That probably hasn't changed too much today either. But when Mary let down her hair, it was not just her hair coming down but also her glory. She was becoming undone at the feet of Jesus.

When you let down your glory at the feet of Jesus, his love will always be present. We live in a culture that becomes undone at wanting more money and possessions, at changing how they look to fit in, at other people's opinions. We must take a step back and realize it is at the feet of Jesus where we should be completely undone. Unabandoned. Unashamed. Guilt-free. No striving at his feet, just resting in his love.

Are you undone at the feet of prominence or popularity? Are you undone at the feet of wanting what you can't have? Are you undone at the feet of impatience, and have you taken matters into your own hands because God isn't doing what you want in your timing? Have you become undone at the feet of trying to fix your marriage on your own? Have you become undone by becoming someone you aren't? Whatever you bow to is the very thing that leads you. At the feet of Jesus is the only place worth becoming undone.

David's Descendant

As we read these final verses in Hosea 3, we see that devotion goes to the Lord and to "David's descendant, their king." Bringing in the descendant of David is not just another way of referencing God. In fact, this verse points to Jesus Christ, who would become king through wearing a crown of thorns and taking our place on the cross.

Jesus was born from the bloodline of David. The shocking part is not that Jesus was David's descendant but that Hosea mentions him over seven hundred years before he was born. Hosea and Gomer's story is a love story all about God and his people. Nevertheless, God loves plot twists, and the story is not complete without Jesus. Jesus is the full embodiment of love in human form. Jesus represents every ounce of love that

God has for us. And now we learn that this powerful story of Hosea points to the Man who would come to save the world.

Hosea said God's people would devote their lives to David's descendant, Jesus. In other words, we are not just devoted to the concept of love. That will fall short every time. Our devotion is found in the personification of love, the man Jesus Christ. For Jesus not only defines love; he is love. It is Jesus to whom we run in our moments of chaos and meltdowns. It is Jesus to whom we look for how to live in this world with God's love. It is Jesus and only Jesus.

Hosea pointed to the coming Messiah hundreds of years before Jesus ever got to earth. We have the advantage of being on the other side of history and get to live in the days after he gave his life. So what will you do with this chance at a new life and a redeeming love? For Hosea and the people of Israel, love was yet to come. For you and me, love has arrived, and his name is Jesus.

Tremble

I used to think God was an old man with a big white beard who sat on a massive throne with a lightning bolt in his hand. A bit like Santa Claus, I guess. I was young and did not understand who God is, but I sure thought he was great at judgments. He is, don't misunderstand. But I never knew he was so much more.

I thought God was ready to strike me the moment I got anything wrong. The fact that I got it wrong a whole lot and was never struck down should have been my hint. But this was my strange view of God—that he only loved me when I was good. When I would hear the command to "fear the Lord," I legit was scared of him. No joke. I did not realize that to fear the Lord means to be in awe of his greatness. This crazy perspective of God caused me to lead my life in a fear-based manner, trying not to sin so I could make God happy with me.

This may sound weird, but there are many people who have a similar view of God. Their view may not be of a big, bad judge like mine was, but it is unhealthy nonetheless. Maybe you still let rules slip into your daily routine because your religion is stronger than your relationship. Possibly you try hard to be who God wants you to be, trying to change yourself without ever going to him and letting him change you. Do you believe that God loves you more when you don't sin? These are all perspectives that will lead you away from the intimate relationship you are called to have with Christ.

But let me ask you, What are you in awe of? What captures your attention more than anything else? What steals away your heart from the moments of life? What takes you out of your regularly scheduled life and into another realm? Is it entertainment? Is it your kids? Is it your favorite hobby? Is it an achievement you desire to reach? What grabs your imagination? These are very important questions to answer as they will lead you to who or what gets your best.

Living in awe of God is the call of every heart. To be stunned by his goodness. To be floored by grace. To be in shock that God knows your name. To live in a constant state of gratitude because of all that God has done for you and who he is to you. To live in awe is to live a life full of color.

The last line of Hosea's story says, "In the last days, they will tremble in awe of the LORD and of his goodness" (3:5 NLT).

Even after Gomer got it all wrong, the story ends with people being in awe of God.

I used to tremble in awe of God's wrath as I thought he would obliterate me from the earth. I trembled in awe of God's judgment against me; I just could not get things right and would always fall back into sin, thinking I had lost God's love. I had convinced myself that God disapproved of me, and I trembled in awe of his disapproval. I trembled in awe of God for all of the wrong reasons, which led me to a toxic faith. One that was works-based. One that was fear-based. But I got it all wrong. We must not be in awe of our sin or God's wrath. No, friends. We must tremble in awe of God and his goodness.

How beautiful is that? We are called to look to the goodness of God. Think back to every moment God's goodness got you to where you are today. It is God's goodness that has spared you in those moments you were about to go off the rails. God's goodness came through for you every time, and yet you wonder whether his goodness has departed from you because of how you are living. Were you living perfectly back then when his goodness showed itself? Not at all.

Friends, it is not our perfection but his that causes us to be in awe of such goodness. It is by his goodness that we can come boldly to his throne of grace when we are in need. It is by his goodness that we woke up today, breathed another breath, and saw another day. Start looking at his goodness, not your badness. You become what you focus on the most. What if you zeroed in on God's goodness more than anything else? You would know you are loved, called, highly favored, not forgotten, and powerful in the hands of God.

God is good. He has always been good, he is good, and he will always be good. His goodness and love go hand in hand. He's good to you because he loves you. He loves you because he is so good. Brennan Manning once said, "We should be astonished at the goodness of God, stunned that He should bother to call us by name, our mouths wide open at His love, bewildered that at this very moment we are standing on holy ground."[6]

Here are some Scriptures that reveal the depth and truth of God's love and goodness.

Then He said, "I will make all My goodness pass before you, and I will proclaim the name of the LORD before you. I will be gracious to whom I will be gracious, and I will have compassion on whom I will have compassion." (Exod. 33:19 NKJV)

Surely goodness and mercy and unfailing love shall fol-
    low me all the days of my life,
And I shall dwell forever [throughout all my days] in
    the house and in the presence of the LORD. (Ps. 23:6
    AMP)

I'm sure now I'll see God's goodness
    in the exuberant earth.
Stay with GOD!
    Take heart. Don't quit.
I'll say it again:
    Stay with GOD. (Ps. 27:13–14)

How great is Your goodness,
Which You have stored up for those who [reverently]
    fear You,

Which You have prepared for those who take refuge in
You,
Before the sons of man! (Ps. 31:19 AMP)

Taste and see that the LORD is good.
Oh, the joys of those who take refuge in him!
(Ps. 34:8 NLT)

Give thanks to the LORD, for he is good;
his love endures forever. (Ps. 107:1 NIV)

Be good to your servant, GOD;
be as good as your Word.
Train me in good common sense;
I'm thoroughly committed to living your way.
(Ps. 119:65–66)

You are good, and the source of good;
train me in your goodness. (Ps. 119:68)

The LORD is good to all;
he has compassion on all he has made.
(Ps. 145:9 NIV)

"I know what I'm doing. I have it all planned out—plans
to take care of you, not abandon you, plans to give you the
future you hope for.

"When you call on me, when you come and pray to me, I'll
listen.

"When you come looking for me, you'll find me.

"Yes, when you get serious about finding me and want it
more than anything else, I'll make sure you won't be disappointed." GOD's Decree.

"I'll turn things around for you. I'll bring you back from all the countries into which I drove you"—GOD's Decree—"bring you home to the place from which I sent you off into exile. You can count on it." (Jer. 29:11–14)

Stay with God. Be fully devoted to his love. God's got this. Live unmasked and undone.

EXPIRATION DATE

11

God's love is like an ocean. You can see its beginning,
but not its end.

Rick Warren

Have you ever thought about how so many things in our
world have an expiration date? Almost every item at the
grocery store has an expiration date stamped on it; one day that
item will be past the point of safe consumption. Have you ever
accidentally—or purposely on a ridiculous dare—drank old,
expired milk? It's the worst! And I am not sorry for bringing
this memory back to you.

Have you realized that one day we too will expire? Our life
is not a permanent gift. We are guests in this world, looking
forward to heaven being our eternal home. We are on borrowed
breath. We are living within unstoppable time. We cannot re-
play the past and we cannot fast-forward to our future, because
the only thing we have been promised is today. Did you catch

that? Today is literally all we have. It is interesting how most of our anxieties are birthed from thoughts about tomorrow. However, this is the day God made, so let's make something great out of it.

All that to say, the human life has an expiration date. Live life to the fullest today. Do not wait for tomorrow to make the changes that could improve your now. If you are waiting for your emotions to line up with your disciplines, you may be waiting for a very long time. Oftentimes you must decide to change before you feel like doing it. Live your best life now by stepping away from your past and deciding to never go back to who you used to be.

Even our emotions expire. Feelings are fleeting things that we buy into. Emotions then begin to disguise themselves as truth. When we start listening to our emotions, we even weigh them against the voice of God. It then becomes difficult to discern which voice is leading you—your own or God's? However, if you have lived longer than a few months, you will realize that most emotions fade away. Sure, you may still be able to feel the hurt you've experienced in your past, or you remember a loved one who passed away or that high school sweetheart who broke your heart. Nevertheless, most emotions are here one minute, gone the next. And I encourage you to get over old hurts; your future is never found in your past.

Love is an emotion. An intense emotion, but an emotion nonetheless. As humans we often live from emotion to emotion. Then we somehow think if we find love within a relationship, we will not be so emotionally unstable. This is true for both men and women. We ride that roller coaster of emotions and cannot seem to get off the ride. It makes us sick. It gets us dizzy. We don't know which way is up or down. We don't know what is right or wrong. We are lost in a sea of feelings. This intense, powerful sensation of love knocks on your door and you open it—and find the person of your dreams. You've been waiting all your life for this person. You look into their eyes, and after the first date you know that this is your future staring back at you. You have hawks, not butterflies, in your stomach every time you think about this person. You're sure you've found happily ever after.

Fast-forward through the engagement and wedding, and now you've been married for some years. You realize that you may have underestimated how messy this person is. It's possible you overlooked that they may not be the person you expected. But isn't that the beauty of marriage? Marriage is a constant challenge of growth and communication. Then comes the thought: "I know I love my husband, but I am not feeling that right now as I look at him sitting on the couch while I clean the house"; or, "I for sure love my wife, but it just feels different than when we first got married. We were passionate back then."

These are normal thoughts. However, they show us that emotions do fade. They will expire. The beauty of love within a marriage is that love grows beyond mere emotion; it becomes a choice. When you say "I do" on your wedding day, that is not the last time you have to say yes to your marriage. You constantly have to say yes to your love for each other. And even though married love is incredible, it is only temporary. Still, by consistently choosing to say yes, you can stand the test of time.

Love between a man and a woman—even love between two best friends—seems to change and alter as life goes on.

This is not the kind of love that lasts, as the story of Hosea illustrates. Love that lasts is not found in anything with an expiration date. No food, no addiction, and no relationship will give you the long-term satisfaction your soul desperately searches for. And what you need more than anything else is not what you've been wanting. What you need is a real dose of something that lasts.

We live in a world where everything is built on a fleeting foundation. Anything we gain from this world is only temporary. Stop searching for eternal answers from a fading world.

Every day when we wake up, we continue our search. Our life has become a rhythm of compromise, and we are stuck in monotony. We repeat our past, hoping that it will create something fresh for our future. We hope we will win the lottery to give us a better life. We stare at social media countless hours a day, hoping someone will like what we shared. We go to church to show people that we have a sense of morality and spirituality. We smile with our face, yet in our heart we feel disgraced. We struggle with anxiety yet only tell people that God is good. Yes, God is good, but are we? Depression seems to win the battle of our thought life, and by nine in the morning we are already emotionally done with our day. Yet we still continue on our way, thinking things will magically get better. We're trying to find the eternal in what is momentary. Stop living from moment to moment. We are called to live from glory to glory.

You will find whatever you are looking for. If you can define what you are searching for, you can identify the direction your life is headed.

Ask, and it will be given to you; seek, and you will find; knock, and it will be opened to you. For everyone who asks receives, and the one who seeks finds, and to the one who knocks it will be opened. (Matt. 7:7–8 ESV)

The context of this passage is Jesus teaching about persistence in prayer and explaining how our Father in heaven knows how to give good gifts to his children. But I want to look at it from a slightly different angle. What if God is also saying that you will find whatever you keep seeking after? I am not saying that God wants to give you temporary pleasures, but if that is all you ask for, God may hand you over to that desire. If you keep knocking on a door of personal gratification, you may get just that. You will be happy for a moment, only to realize in the end that the pleasure was empty.

This is where we become deceived by the attraction to fake. We think it's what we need, then realize it only results in emptiness. Worldly pleasures look fulfilling to the eye yet leave us wanting more every time. Saying yes to sin and expecting satisfaction is like watching the food channel and expecting to be full by the end of the show. You will end up frustrated and will have to deal with the same hunger pains you always had, because you misdiagnosed your needs. It's an illusion that humanity is buying into. In Christ are pleasures forevermore, and those are the only pleasures that will fill your soul.

Genesis 4:7 pictures sin as hiding behind a door: "If you do what is right, will you not be accepted? But if you do not do what is right, sin is crouching at your door; it desires to have you, but you must rule over it" (NIV). We need discernment.

We need to distinguish the voice of God from the voices that would lead us astray. So be careful about the door you knock on—you may get what you never wanted. However, if you keep knocking on the door of God's heart, you will find everything you need, everything you did not even know you needed, and more.

The only thing that will not expire in your life is the love of God. Living this truth is easier said than done. We have lost sight of the love of God. Despite reassurances that "God loves us," we fail to realize that God's love is intensely personal. We talk about the love of God as if it were a reality meant for others when it should be very personal and real for each of us.

Once we get our eyes off of the temporal, we can see that God's love for us is eternal. Romans 8:38–39 powerfully declares that nothing can or will separate us from the eternal, long-lasting love of Jesus. Yet, how often do we feel separated from this love? All the time! I am a pastor, and even I admit that there are times I do not sense this love. It is because we are emotional beings searching for fulfillment. Nevertheless, the truth still stands that God's love never leaves you. Even if you do not see it or recognize it, the love of Jesus is always around you.

It's a perspective issue. It's not that God's love is gone; it's that our eyes have wandered. The only reason you cannot see something is because you are not looking at it.

Here is a good practice: When you don't feel loved, tell yourself you're loved. When you don't see God's love, declare his love over your life. When you are in a dark moment, remind yourself you are not alone. When you are struggling, think about the goodness of God's love and watch him pull you through.

Love that lasts is only found in the One who has lasted from generation to generation.

God's Love + My Desires = Fulfillment

So often we think that additives make things better. Whenever I order an iced tea, I need sugar and lemons to make it better. Whenever I eat chicken nuggets (something I rarely do because I'm a grown man), I need dipping sauce. We are constantly trying to improve the quality of something through additives. We do this because the current offering is not up to our liking. If it is not exactly how we want it, we want something extra.

We live in a world addicted to additives. These additives make everything we consume better. These additions improve the quality of the moment—or so we think. And if we are not careful, we will bring our additives mind-set into the presence of God. We will begin to tell ourselves things like, "The love of God is enough for me only if it produces the man of my dreams" or "The love of God is all I need only if it leads me to prosperity."

We have bought into a version of life that always wants something more. The problem is that God needs no additives. He needs nothing else. God alone is God enough. God sent his Son, Jesus, to take away the sins of the world. Jesus hung on a cross that he did not deserve. After three days he rose from the grave, defeating sin, death, and hell. This is unbelievable stuff! And he did it because God so loved the world.

Many of us bring a dangerous additive into our relationship with Jesus, and that is the attitude of entitlement. We all, at some point in our lives, have felt entitled for God to make something happen on our behalf. For example, if you've had a tough upbringing, you may feel entitled for God to offset that by giving you an easy adulthood. We feel entitled whenever we believe God owes us something or needs to do more for us. Entitlement ends when we realize that God owes us nothing because he has already given us everything!

On the cross, Jesus declared, "It is finished." Whenever we attempt to add anything that is not of or from Jesus to our lives, we are telling him that what he did on the cross was not enough. We often want salvation *and* a nice car. We want redemption *and* a relationship with someone. We want the Messiah *but also* that miracle we've been asking for. We easily fall into the trap of discontentment.

Discontentment tells you, "God is mostly enough—now let's fill those other empty spaces in your soul with what you want." Our prayer life becomes riddled with our desires. We drink the communion cup on Sunday, thanking God for his sacrifice, only to be unsatisfied on Monday with all that he has not done for us.

Psalm 37:4 says, "Delight yourself in the LORD, and he will give you the desires of your heart" (ESV). I don't know about you, but I used to get so excited about this verse. I would read about how God was going to give me the desires of my heart, and it would put an immediate smile on my face. Who wouldn't be thrilled that God was going to hook them up with all that they wanted? Every day is like Christmas morning with Jesus! But then I started to realize that God wasn't giving me every desire that I've ever wanted, so I started to carefully read and study this passage.

The verse begins by giving us a statement, a command if you will: "Delight yourself in the LORD." Delight means to please greatly. The Contemporary English Version even translates this as, "Do what the LORD wants." This first half of the verse calls us to think differently—to live on God's terms and do things God's way. This verse empowers believers to seek first the kingdom of God. Once you start living according to God's desires, your desires will change. What is important to God is now important to you. What breaks God's heart now breaks yours. What brings joy to Jesus now brings joy to you! It is a paradigm shift to live in the rhythm of God's desires.

Once that becomes your lifestyle, your own personal wants are no longer what they used to be. Psalm 37:4 is not saying that God will give you your casual wants and wishes from time to time. This verse is stating that once you live in God's ways, your desires will be shaped and formed around God's will for your life. Your prayer life will change. You will find yourself asking for things that have an eternal impact instead of a personal improvement. God will replace your wants with his desires.

With that understanding, we recognize that adding our wants to what God is doing would be a mistake of epic proportions. We would be missing the ball that is sitting on a tee. Our call is not to add to the love of God but to receive it in full and find that we need nothing more, nothing less.

Let's look at the first verse of Psalm 23. I have included it for you here in two different translations.

> The LORD is my shepherd;
> I shall not want. (NKJV)

The LORD is my shepherd, I lack nothing. (NIV)

Once again the Bible gives us a two-part Scripture in the form of cause and effect. There is a cure to our culture's "want" disease, and that is to have a shepherd. There is a mandate for believers to have a shepherd, to have someone to lead and guide us. That shepherd cannot be anyone or anything but Jesus.

It is so easy to let money, marriage, possessions, influence, and temporary love become our shepherd. Later we realize that these things do not last. Your life is a direct result of where you've put your trust and who or what you've allowed to shepherd you. Make no mistake about it, the Lord is your shepherd. If he's not, you need to change that. The longer God is not guiding and protecting your life, the more difficult it will be for you to overcome the attitude of demanding him to do more.

When God takes his rightful role in your life as shepherd, guide, leader, and protector, you can overcome your struggle of wanting more. When God is in control, you lack nothing. Wherever you are in life, no matter the season, you can be free from trying to bring additives to God's call for your life.

Choose the love that lasts. Don't settle for something that expires, only to find yourself unfulfilled and joyless. Jesus is all you need, and he will last the test of time.

12

TRUST. RECEIVE. RELEASE.

For the LORD your God is living among you.
    He is a mighty savior.
He will take delight in you with gladness.
    With his love, he will calm all your fears.
He will rejoice over you with joyful songs.

Zephaniah 3:17 NLT

My two-year-old son loves almond milk. We started giving him almond milk early on due to a slight dairy allergy, but he grew to love it. One day he asked me for some milk—a basic request that happens on a daily basis. So I went to the fridge and pulled out the almond milk, then went to the cupboard and pulled out one of his kid cups. Out of nowhere, Beckham began to cry and scream. Thinking that it was for the milk, I quickly poured it into the cup, twisted on the top, and turned around to give it to him. But he kept crying and screaming. So I asked my little boy, "What's wrong, buddy? Here is your milk."

With tears streaming down his little face, Beckham said to me, "I don't want that cup. I want different cup!" And he said it in that exact way as he was yelling.

I tried to have a mature conversation with my two-year-old and told him, "Buddy, it is the same milk; it is just in a different cup. I promise, just try it and you will see that it is your favorite; it's almond milk."

He refused, and at the top of his lungs he yelled, "Daddy, no! Different cup! Different cup!"

There are moments when I stand my ground, but this was not one of them. I quickly went back to the cupboard and poured the milk into the cup he asked for. As I brought it to him, he softly said, "Thank you, Daddy," and I watched him as he happily drank the same milk that he was upset about in the other cup.

I tell you this story because something caught my attention about this entire meltdown moment, as I am sure many of you with kids can relate to. I was struck by the thought that it was the same milk, but my son was hung up over which cup it was going to be in. The milk was what he really wanted and needed more than anything else. The cup was just the delivery system, the container, for something much more important. The cup could not give my son nutrition or satisfy his thirst. Rather, what was in the cup was most important.

My son could not receive the milk because it was not coming to him the way he wanted it to come. He was caught up over how it was being delivered rather than what was being delivered.

What happens when you cannot receive what you need from God because it is not coming the way you thought it should come? How do you respond when you get stuck on God's delivery methods instead of what he is trying to bring you? Do you struggle with how God's going to do something instead of trusting that he will always provide all you need? God wants to get his love through to you, and it may come in the hardest or loneliest season in your life. We miss that it is his love because we are focused on the season instead of the Savior. What if God's love comes to you through people? What if this love is delivered through the channels of challenge? Do not write off what God is pouring out on you and into you just because you don't understand. When you don't understand life, his love is there. When you're caught in a challenge, his love is available. When you're in the midst of a heartbreak, his mending love surrounds you.

Love is uncomfortable to receive when you don't realize it is love that God is trying to give you. Oftentimes when we go to God for love, we have an idea of when and how we should receive it—almost as if God's love package is going to be delivered with blessings and breakthroughs and increases. What if you are missing God's love because you have been looking for a package instead of a person? What happens when you realize that God's love doesn't come with additives or additions? It comes like a fire and it takes over, but don't expect it to come in line with your preconceptions. When love comes, it encompasses and surrounds. It is not a love that comes with blessings, because the love of God is the greatest blessing to our souls.

My son missed the fact that the style of cup did not change the quality of the contents. God wants to get his love to you however you will receive it. And the truth of the matter is that we all receive a little differently depending on how we were brought up by our parents or guardians. My son wanted milk, but in his own way. He is two and no one can blame him for that. But you and me? We should know better. Wanting God's love in our own way to our own benefit reveals that we are spiritual toddlers.

Let's go further with this thought. How often do we want God to prove his love to us? And how often do we question God's love because of the inhumane situations that persist in our world? It is like God is on trial and we are prosecuting him for not fixing everything. Just because evil exists doesn't mean his love is distant. Just because bad things happen does not mean good is gone. We must not tie together pervasive evil and abounding love. Love does not control because love is a choice. So for you to ask God to prove his love is a silly request. He already did that on the cross. For us to view his love as the mechanic to fix our worldly issues is also flawed thinking. Love needs a vessel to pour into and then flow out of. God's love is all around us; however, love changes everything when it has altered the human heart internally. It is the love of God through us that can change the world. And though chaos is all around, love—real love—is never separated from the hearts of those willing to receive it. Evil may win a battle, but God's love will never lose a war.

Romans 8 compels us not lose sight of God's love when we are going through a battle.

Can anything ever separate us from Christ's love? Does it mean he no longer loves us if we have trouble or calamity, or are persecuted, or hungry, or destitute, or in danger, or threatened with death? (As the Scriptures say, "For your sake we are killed every day; we are being slaughtered like sheep.") No, despite all these things, overwhelming victory is ours through Christ, who loved us. (Rom. 8:35–37 NLT)

His love is not conditional. It does not depend on current circumstances. He loves you on mountain highs and valley lows.

The context of Romans 8 speaks of Jesus's followers losing their lives over their faith. And we thought our problems were intense! These men and women would be killed for admitting to follow Jesus. If I were in that same position, I would be concerned for my life and not thinking, "Is God's love ever separated from me?" Nonetheless, we see devoted followers of Christ who cling desperately to this love. Paul's message here is beautifully real. He is proclaiming that your current situation does not limit the availability of God's perfect love.

What are you going through right now? Is life great? Is life terrible? No matter what you're going through, there is a love that will sustain you through it all. Whether life is good or life is hard, your significance rests in the arms of God.

Blocked Receiver

We have satellite TV in the Berteau household. I don't know how satellite television works. All I know is that the box in my house is called the receiver. When I press the power button on my remote control, this receiver listens and responds accordingly. I press channel up, and guess what? The channel changes! I have no desire to understand how our receiver works. All I know is that it needs to always do its job, which is to receive those signals and put a picture on my screen.

Now that I have impressed you with my technology expertise, let me tell you what happened one rainy day. A storm came in on a Saturday afternoon. We live in Texas, so these storms come quite violently at times. My wife and I are huge college football fans, specifically LSU fans. Geaux Tigers! We were in the middle of the game when suddenly the screen went black and a message popped up that said "Signal loss." I rushed to the rescue to apply my vast knowledge on troubleshooting this technology. I attempted to restart our receiver, but that did not do any good. I then realized that the storm had affected the signal. So there we sat with a blank screen staring us in the face and a storm-blocked receiver.

All I know is that the receiver was unable to receive. There was a storm. An impediment. An obstruction that disabled our receiver from doing what it's meant to do: receive. And when the receiver is hindered in such a way, nothing else connected to it works properly.

God desires for us to receive all that he has to give. We receive his presence. We receive his peace. We receive his joy. We receive his promises for our lives. We receive hope from Christ. We receive a love that is like no other.

Could it be that we sometimes miss what God is giving, not because he is withholding but because our human receiver is being blocked by something? God always has a signal for us to tap into; however, we do not always pick up that signal. Distraction could be the thing blocking you. Broken dreams may be your hindrance. A difficult, stormy season may be impeding your connection.

Is it possible that we know a lot about God's love but don't fully experience it because we struggle to receive or to hear God through the current storm and static? It is time to learn how to have peace in a storm. To keep your eyes on Jesus even though the wind and waves around you are intense. It is time to turn away from your problematic perspective that causes confusion. To put down the distraction so you can start to receive divine love.

Think about a friend who struggles to receive a gift on their birthday or at Christmas. They may feel insecure, unworthy of this celebratory moment. Or maybe you have a friend who becomes awkward whenever you give them a compliment. Because they do not feel worthy of the compliment, they hear it but don't receive it as their own.

Many of us do the same thing every time God tries to give us something. He attempts to give us love, yet we feel unworthy, so we walk away. Friends, our receivers are impaired and need to be adjusted as soon as possible. There is a word from God coming in, but we cannot hear it through the distractions. There is restorative love coming from heaven, but we won't drop our guilt or shame long enough to see that God is for us, not against us. And guess what? Since God is not against you, the only one who is really against you is you. Yes, Satan is technically against you, but the only one who can stop you is you. Your biggest critic is you. Right this moment you can tune back in to heaven's frequency and realize that nothing can stop your pursuit to hear the voice of God. Draw near to him and he will always draw near to you (James 4:8).

Perhaps your receiver has no signal because of what happened to you in your past. Maybe someone knows. Maybe no one knows. And you cannot receive from God because all you can think about is this unhealed pain that has yet to be addressed in your life. You cannot even receive God's forgiveness for your past, because you fail to forgive yourself for what has happened. Yes, it happened. However, do not let what's happened in your past stop you from receiving God in your present. Your receiver—your heart and soul—is restored by the great Redeemer, as long as you are willing to walk down the road of wholeness.

Your receiver isn't working because you view your heavenly Father like you view your earthly father. This is a big one. Our earthly fathers are not perfect. They are all human. Maybe you had no father figure growing up, and the wounds from that upbringing are too deep. It is easier for you to leave them untouched. Perhaps you had a dad who was physically present but emotionally absent. He was not there for your needs. He did not cheer you on in your schooling or sports. You never felt that fatherly support from your earthly father.

If we had a negative experience with our earthly father, we often transfer those negative issues onto God. This hurts our spiritual growth and our walk with God. We place God in the same category as a father who failed us, was absent, was never there for us, never believed in us, never prayed with us, and so on. Even if you had a great dad, like I did, you cannot place these earthly limitations on an infinitely good heavenly Father. Father God is not your earthly dad—whether you had a great one, a bad one, or none at all. The beautiful picture that needs to be painted in your mind is that in every moment of weakness, in your breakdowns and meltdowns, in those moments you would cry yourself to sleep at night, in those times you wanted someone to be proud of you, God was there every step of the way. He is the perfect Father you may have never known you had.

Maybe you have difficulty receiving the love of your heavenly Father because you never had a chance to receive any kind of love from your earthly dad or guardian. You could be in your thirties, forties, fifties—really any age—and still feel the deep impact and loss of never having love shown to you from a parental figure. Nevertheless, God is Abba Father. When Jesus prayed, he often used the word *Abba*, one of the most intimate names for "Dad." You have never been alone. You have always had a Father. It is time to adjust your receiver to find saving love in the always open arms of Father God.

Your receiver could be hindered for a million different reasons. Is there a persisting sin in your life? Have you misdefined love as lust, continually chasing temporary pleasures only to find yourself emptier each time? Even if you were raised in church, like I was, perhaps love is more of a concept than a reality. If you have not encountered God in a long time, it is not God's fault. God is always watching over you with compassion and love and is waiting for you to draw near. To fix your receiver, you have to get on God's frequency. He is constantly speaking. The Holy Spirit is consistently guiding. Are you steadily listening?

Jesus does not need your approval in order to love you. God loves you despite what you feel has disqualified you. Stop fighting against the very thing that will change your existence. Let this love break down your walls and infiltrate your heart. Let this love pierce your life like it did his hands and feet on the cross. Let God in. Let Jesus obliterate your past and call you his own. Start believing whatever God calls you.

When God calls you his child, believe it. You are not an unloved orphan. You have a home.

When God calls you a conqueror, walk in it. You are more than a conqueror in Christ.

When God calls you an overcomer, take it to heart.

When God calls you a victor, immediately cease wallowing in defeat. You win.

When God calls you blessed, thank him with great gratitude.

When God calls you a world changer, go change the world with no regrets.

When God calls you forgiven, don't let shame steal your connection with Jesus.

When God calls you anxiety-free, live without a worry in the world.

When God calls you healed, stop questioning. Start trusting.

When God calls you whole, walk securely, knowing your empty days are done.

When God calls you redeemed, realize your debt has been paid in full and you are a new creation.

When God calls you restored, believe that your wounds are now your testimony.

When God calls you to go, don't wait one moment. Walk on that water in front of you.

When God calls you loved, receive it. You are his beloved. He is head over heels for you.

What God calls you is what should define you. And what he has called you cannot be undone by the works of the enemy. The enemy lies because he knows if you figure out who you are and what is inside of you, no devil in hell can stop you from impacting this world. The moment you learn to receive from God, you can no longer receive the enemy's lies. The devil's days are over in your life, so serve him an eviction notice. Let him know you are not for sale. Your receiver is working, and you just got a fresh download of real love. And now that you have this game-changing love, it will change everything about you and around you.

When you're not good enough, God is.

When you're deeply hurt, he heals.

When you want to quit, he sustains.

When you are weak, he's your strength.

When you are lost, he is your home.

When you feel worthless, he calls you worthy.

When you feel forgotten, he knows your name.

When you feel overlooked, he chooses you.

When you call yourself inadequate, he says you are perfectly crafted.

When you don't measure up, he picks you up.

When you are hopeless, he is your very hope.

When you are suicidal, he's your abundant life.

When you feel unloved, he is your unfiltered, immeasurable love.

When you say, "I can't be loved," he says you already are.

LOVE HAS A RHYTHM

13

Are you tired? Worn out? Burned out on religion? Come to me. Get away with me and you'll recover your life. I'll show you how to take a real rest. Walk with me and work with me—watch how I do it. *Learn the unforced rhythms of grace.* I won't lay anything heavy or ill-fitting on you. Keep company with me and you'll learn to live freely and lightly.

Matthew 11:28–30, emphasis added

When you find real love, you find more than just love. Discovering God's love for your life is a powerful moment. However, you just received more than perfect love. Along with this life-altering love, you now have the ability to walk in a rhythm with God. Not just a balance; a rhythm.

Have you ever met anyone who has no rhythm? Or maybe you are that person? Nowadays dance moves have become complicated. I'm on the younger end of life, but still, today's new moves are interesting. I'm just going to stay in my lane and keep doing the Running Man. And if the moment calls for it, I always have that specialty called the Worm. If you have no idea what I'm talking about, thank God for Google. However, when that certain song comes on—and we all have a trigger song that gets us up and moving—many people have much more confidence than rhythm.

Rhythm may be optional when it comes to the dance floor, but it's indispensable when it comes to living in God's love and purpose. Walking with God comes with a rhythm for living your life. Don't attempt to find your spiritual stride by yourself. We get ourselves in trouble when we search worldly places, possessions, and personal achievements for the tempo that only God can give. God is the source of your next steps, and he sets a pace of grace for your life.

Let's look back to the beginning, to when God made Adam's wife and helper, Eve. Let's see if we can identify God's rhythm.

> The Lord God said, "It is not good for the man to be alone. I will make a helper suitable for him." Now the Lord God had formed out of the ground all the wild animals and all the birds in the sky. He brought them to the man to see what he would name them; and whatever the man called each living creature, that was its name. So the man gave names to all the livestock, the birds in the sky and all the wild animals. But for Adam no suitable helper was found. So the Lord God caused the man to fall into a deep sleep; and while he was sleeping, he took one of the man's ribs and then closed up the place with flesh. Then the Lord God made a woman from the rib he had taken out of the man, and he brought her to the man. (Gen. 2:18–22 NIV)

This is the first time in the Bible where God says something is "not good." It was not good for Adam to be alone.

Now, this is not a universal statement that we automatically apply to any and all lifestyles. No, loneliness is not good for you. And even if you are married, you can absolutely still feel the bitter bite of loneliness. Also, know that being alone and loneliness are two different things. If you are alone, you can learn how to be content and discern the voice of God. Loneliness is not the result of being alone but of not letting God fill that missing void. Married people know that marriage is not the antidote to loneliness. No other person can fill the emptiness that plagues our souls. Don't put that pressure on another human being. Fulfillment is the job of the Almighty; submission is our job.

When God said it was not good for Adam to be alone, he was talking about a man who was already walking with him and trusting him. If you read the preceding verses, you will see that Adam was tending, cultivating, and watching over the garden before Eve was ever on the scene. Adam was called to do something before he was given someone. He had a calling before he had a companion. This reveals a particular rhythm when it comes to our search for love, whether we're single or married: you have a calling before you have a companion.

If you are married, you still have a calling even though you have your companion. Your calling was not handed in at the altar on your wedding day. When you said "I do" and the two became one, your callings also came together.

Genesis 2:18–22 reveals four steps in God's rhythm for our lives. It is a rhythm in which God calls for his people to know and trust him. When we live in the real love of God, like Adam was doing, we will discover that: (1) God brings what's next; (2) God lets you name it; (3) God's working on it; and (4) God extracts purpose from pain.

God brings what's next. In Genesis 2, we see that God brought the animals to Adam so that he could name them. God had made a promise that he was going to create a helper for Adam, but first he brought him a process of naming animals. Yes, in Adam's mind he may have been looking for his helpmate; but as we all know, he was not going to find her among the animal kingdom. Promises from God are almost always followed by a process from God.

The season of process often tests us in life and in God's love. We want everything to be immediate. We want to have what we need when we think we need it. However, life with God means trusting that God's timing is always perfect.

God also brought Eve to Adam. Adam did not force the situation and become impatient; he allowed God to bring him whatever was next for his life. Adam allowed God to be God. What a powerful truth. It is one thing to realize you are loved by relentless, perfect love. It is another thing when you let that love of God rule your heart and mind. God brought the process and the promise to Adam. This is a piece of God's rhythm that we must not ignore: God will bring you what is next.

God lets you name it. When God brought the animals to Adam, God wanted him to name them. This was Adam exercising the dominion that God gave him. The Bible says that whatever Adam named an animal, that's what it was called. So whatever name came out of Adam's mouth, it stuck.

God brings you what is next, and then in his rhythm, he allows you to name what is in front of you. For example, you used to call your husband an answer to prayer, but now you call him a lazy father. God brought you a process but you called it a storm. God brought you a season to be alone with him and find contentment, but you called it loneliness and depression.

You see, whatever you call it, that's what it is. The power of life and death is in your tongue, and you have the dominion and authority to name situations as they should be. It is time to take inventory of your life and go back and rename some things. What you called a season of trial needs to be renamed a season of development. What you called a curse may in fact be a blessing. Maybe you have named God's love as something you will run back to when things get difficult, but you have not named him as a priority in your life. You have the authority to speak life into your present and your future.

God also said he wanted to "see" what Adam would call the animals. There is a revelation here that you will end up seeing whatever you start saying. No, I am not speaking about a "get rich quick" or "name it, claim it" type of living. This is more of a perspective challenge.

Say a new thing. Say a better thing. Speak God's love over your life. Speak abundance into your household. Speak peace and restoration into your marriage. Speak life where there is death. Even if you do not physically see a difference, do not go back to speaking negatively. When you speak God's heart, your heart will first be changed before the situation changes. Even if your circumstances never change, always speak out the authority of God's word and then trust God to come through.

It is a part of God's rhythm for your life to call things not as they are but as they should be.

Side note: Bible scholars believe that Adam was not only naming animals but looking for his helper. This is why Genesis says that no suitable helper was found once the naming concluded. One reason scholars believe Adam did not find a helper, outside of the obvious, was because the animals he was naming already had mates. So Adam had to name animals while noticing the fact that they had what he lacked—a helper.

If I had been in Adam's position, I would have been frustrated that all the animals had a helper and I didn't. But I believe there is a lesson about contentment here, to be OK with other people having what you do not. This is all a part of God's rhythm. Real love will produce genuine contentment.

God's working on it. After God brought Adam what was next and allowed him to name it, he put Adam into a deep sleep. As Adam slept, the first ever surgery took place. As Adam was sleeping, God was working. What an encouraging thought. And it is true for you today that, even as you lay your head on that pillow and go to sleep, God is still working on your behalf.

> And we know that God works all things together for the good of those who love Him, who are called according to His purpose. (Rom. 8:28 BSB)

Even when you are not thinking of God, he is thinking of you. Even when we are unfaithful, God is still faithful. God is always doing more than we think he is. This is a rhythm that God does not want you to let go of today: he is working out all things, and in the end it will turn out for your good. Trust his love. Trust his presence. He's got this.

God extracts purpose from pain. Once God was done extracting the rib from Adam's side, Adam woke up. If that had happened to me, I would have been wondering why my side was sore. "What just happened to me? Why is my rib missing?" I would ask myself. Now, I am not sure if the perfect environment in the Garden of Eden kept Adam from feeling any residual pain, but he had to at least notice that he was missing something.

Often after God is done working on us, he will remove something from within us. Typically, when God removes something from our lives, he replaces it with something better, something Christ-like. The choice is his. The obedience is ours.

When God extracts something from us, most of the time we experience pain. For example, when a long relationship is removed or when bad habits are cut away, it hurts. It hurts because it was a part of us. However, God must cut some things away for us to move forward.

While Adam may have been wondering what had happened to him, the Bible says that God brought the woman to Adam. Adam was not so caught up in what he lost that he missed what God brought. How often do we get stuck on what we do not have or what we lost instead of trusting that God will be faithful to complete the good work he started in us? Maybe you do not have what you want because it is not what you need. Just because you see God working in someone else's life does not mean he has forgotten about you. He may be working in their life, but he may be working something out of yours.

I remember when I had to go get a mole on my back checked to see if it was cancerous. It is never a pleasant doctor's visit when it has to do with a major issue like cancer. My wife and I went in the room and the doctor began inspecting my back. He did not have a conclusive answer and recommended removing the mole just in case. That threw us a bit because we thought for sure this would not be malignant. Now, I am a tough guy, but I would prefer if everything on my body stayed on my body. For the sake of safety, however, I decided to go ahead with the procedure. As the man was sawing off part of my back, I thought to myself, "There has to be a better way to do this with modern medicine and advanced technology." However, it took a knife to remove that mole from my back.

I tell you this story because there had to be a removal for us to have certainty. Who knows what might have happened if I had left that mole on my back? Because I had it removed, I knew it would cause me no harm. I was sore for at least a couple weeks after that procedure; however, the pain did not outweigh the certainty and comfort I felt knowing the threat was gone.

When God removes something from your life, it is for a purpose. For Adam, that purpose was Eve. Even though taking a rib out would be a painful procedure, the promise of God made the pain worth it. When we go through pain, God uses it for a purpose.

Out of Adam's side came his bride, Eve. When Jesus was on the cross, one of the final things the soldier did was stab his side with a spear. Blood and water flowed out of Jesus's side, completely emptying him out. Just like Eve was extracted from the side of Adam, salvation for humanity was extracted from the side of Jesus.

Jesus endured extreme pain for us. However, he endured it for the joy set before him. That joy is you and me. Out of the side of Jesus came purpose. Whatever you are walking through right now and no matter the pain level, God will always extract purpose from your pain. He loves you way too much to waste your hurt.

Where's the Balance?

When real love finds you, it finds you just as you are and right where you are. This means that love does not only bring balance to your life, it brings fulfillment. I'm not talking about just any love that finds you; I'm talking about the love of Christ.

Everyone is busy. The fact that you are sitting and reading this book right now is a miracle because of how busy our lives have become. We have kids' games to attend, school papers to write, full-time jobs, church life, friendships, date nights, and thirty-six unread text messages. Life is crazy busy. Where does God's love figure in when it comes to how intense some of our lives are?

I remember watching an Olympic gymnastics event called the balance beam. In this competition, elegant humans get on a beam about four inches wide and do a routine. All while staying on top of this beam. This particular competition has to be one of the more unique events I've ever seen.

Now, the goal is to first stay on the beam. If you fall off, points are deducted. However, the way to get a high score is not just by staying on. The way to win is by finding a rhythm.

This balance beam is a lot like life. We are attempting to walk through life at a pace where we can still control everything. We are trying to find balance. But how can we find something we cannot identify? Does balance mean your house is clean and the kids are cared for? Does balance mean your bills are all being paid? Is balance graduating college and getting married? If everyone has a different definition of balance, then you will find no absolute on which to balance your life. You may find a place where you feel balanced for a few weeks. Nevertheless, something always comes and knocks you off, or you're given some responsibility and struggle to integrate into your life.

If you could find full balance, you would not need God. If your life was always in order, you would not need God to help and direct you. This is why I am convinced that life is not about balance, it is about rhythm. When the love of God meets you, it gives you a new rhythm and pace in life. You have a different bounce in your step when you know the love of God always has your back. And the moment life gets overwhelming, which it will, love will sustain you through that trial. God's love does not remove the difficult circumstances you are going through; it carries you through them.

We need to be OK with not being OK. Stop hiding your life when everything is out of balance. Those who seem like they have everything under control often have nothing under control. Everyone wants to convince people that they have this elusive balanced life; they never show the world who they really are. However, God's grace is sufficient, and his strength is made perfect in your weakness.

You may have too much on your plate. Your schedule may be too full. You may be overcommitted. Nonetheless, God's love affirms that he is with you in every step and every breath.

So go ahead and take on those dreams and aspirations God has given you. Rest in his rhythm and experience a life that only his love could produce—a life of validation, affirmation, and confidence in Jesus Christ.

LOVE RULES

God's greatest attribute is not his power, though it is omniscience; not his glory, though it is burning majesty: it is his love.

Al Bryant

Don't lose your grip on Love and Loyalty.
Tie them around your neck; carve their initials on your heart.

Proverbs 3:3

Love does not magically change things in your life. It does not do the work for you. Love is an altering agent that must be received and applied. Love has to be in charge. Once this love is in you, then it can do work within you. Once it is working within you, it must come out of you. You are not loved just so you can walk around being loved. You are loved so you can be love. The places where love does not reach go unchanged.

Don't lose your grip on love. Tie it around your neck and carve it in your heart. This is strong language to illustrate the importance of love making its mark on us. Love is something you choose when you wake up and do not feel your best. You choose this love because it is ingrained in who you are. You cannot let go of this love once it has hit you and overwhelmed you.

You will never fully understand God's love; that is not a part of humanity's job description. We must stop griping about what we don't understand and start gripping on to what gives us hope. Love must reach the inner being of who we are. Love must leak into our consciousness so it becomes second nature to live in this manner. Love must be allowed to go where it needs to go and do what it needs to do.

Love won't go where you don't let it. You may have an incredible relationship with God. You may feel his presence on a daily basis and pursue his heart constantly. But for some reason you still seem to find yourself in compromised moments, fighting to fill an emptiness that you know only God can fill. What is it about our human nature that causes even Christians to know about love but not let it do work in our lives? I have found that even when I have a great relationship with God, I often make his love Plan B and give relational love higher priority.

Maybe you have yet to allow this love in your dating life. So you pursue what you want because you know you can always go back to God if your plan does not work. What a hopeless way to live, asking God to approve your plans for your life. Instead, if love took over your dating life, your standards would be so high, you would pass at any chance of compromise. Love changes the dating game.

Love can change your marriage. Maybe you are a husband with wandering eyes. Whatever you look at will become the way you think. The way you think will become the way you live. So be careful what you view, for your vision is the window to your soul. Husbands, has real love taken over your wandering eyes? It cannot change what you will not allow it to. The reason you think the grass is greener on the other side is because you have been staring at someone else's lawn while not tending your own.

Love will rock you at your core. It shows those of us who deal with lust that impurity is an invitation to heartbreak. Impurity will keep you longer than you are willing to stay and cost you more than you are willing to pay. Start to use your eyes to look at the blessings around you. When you lust, it is because you are wanting something or someone that is not yours. Lust is from the pit of hell and is tearing marriages apart on a daily basis. Pornography will prove to be detrimental to your godly union. Impure thoughts running rampant will lead you down a path of regret. Chasing a temporary pleasure will always lead you to a disappointing finish.

> God is love. When we take up permanent residence in a life of love, we live in God and God lives in us. This way, love has the run of the house, becomes at home and mature in us, so that we're free of worry on Judgment Day—our standing in the world is identical with Christ's. (1 John 4:17)

The only way love wins is when love rules. Love is not a place you visit for a short period of time. Love is not only momentary pleasure that gives you an emotional high. Love does not give you what you want. Love is what you need.

Who really runs your house? Who sits on the throne of your heart and calls the shots? Who is actually in charge of your decision-making? If God is not in charge, you are destined for a letdown. We are not built to sustain ourselves. You cannot love yourself enough to the point of fulfillment and satisfaction. If you could, those feelings would be fleeting. Who is the real authority in your life? Are God's love and grace nothing more than a bail-out plan to your unchanging ways? Love must have the keys to your house and the authority to guide you forward.

The Most Important Commandment

One of the teachers of religious law was standing there listening to the debate. He realized that Jesus had answered well, so he asked, "Of all the commandments, which is the most important?"

Jesus replied, "The most important commandment is this: 'Listen, O Israel! The LORD our God is the one and only LORD. And you must love the LORD your God with all your heart, all your soul, all your mind, and all your strength.' The second is equally important: 'Love your neighbor as yourself.' No other commandment is greater than these." (Mark 12:28–31 NLT)

Isn't it funny how when asked about the Ten Command-ments, Jesus condensed them into two? He could have easily said that all ten were important. However, Jesus came to earth to set a new world order. Jesus wanted to show people that love is not a passing thought but has the leading role in the lives of believers.

This was a major conversation. Jesus was answering not an ignorant bystander but a religious teacher who revered the law. He could have quoted any of the ten commandments in reply— do not commit adultery, do not worship any other gods, do not make idols. All ten are strong options! But in this moment Jesus chose to talk about the most important facet of living in relationship with his Father—love. He encapsulated the entire kingdom of God in two love rules: love God and love people. If that does not reveal to you that love is the heartbeat of all that God is and does, nothing else will.

Let's look at another Scripture passage for even deeper insight into what is most important to God for our lives:

> But for right now, until that completeness, we have three things to do to lead us toward that consummation: Trust steadily in God, hope unswervingly, love extravagantly. And the best of the three is love. (1 Cor. 13:13)

Trust, hope, faith, joy, and any other characteristic of God that we are called to live with are all of vital importance. But as another translation says, "the greatest of these is love" (NIV). This is not to downplay faith or justice by any means. However, God knew he had to point to one characteristic for humanity to grasp hold of.

I felt convicted to write this book because of verses like these. As I look out into society, the church, and Christian culture, I am not convinced that real love is being taught and grasped to the extent Christ calls us to. If love is the greatest of all, it should be a hot topic in our sermons and a constant theme in our relationships. If love is the best of all, we must pray and worship until we encounter something so raw and real from God's throne room that it leaves us unhinged and undone.

This love is real, friends. It is more real than the trees around you or the car you drive. This love carries a message to give our all and draw closer to the heart of our Father. This love is not a fad. It is not just a word that appears on a shirt or necklace and carries minimal meaning. This love cost Jesus the breath in his lungs and the blood in his body. Love sacrificed everything not so we could misinterpret it until we get to the grave. I am not OK with only experiencing God's exponential love after we pass through the gates of heaven and into his perfect presence. I am convinced that your best life is the one led by love. Your best marriage is the one wrapped in love. Your only way to experience contentment and fulfillment in singleness is with this love carved on your heart.

Love is not just something good. Love is everything. Love wants to rearrange your life and challenge your priorities. Love wants your eyes, ears, mind, and heart. Love will not settle for most of you; it is on a rampage to take all of you. Will you let it? Will you allow love to win the battle for your heart? Love cannot change what it is not allowed to touch in your life. When love rules, love indeed changes everything.

Love changes your perspective.

Love changes your interests.

Love changes your vision.

Love changes your decisions.

Love changes your relationships.

Love changes your confidence.

Love changes your singleness.

Love changes your marriage.

Love changes your friends.

Love changes your wants.

Love changes your endurance.

Love changes your worship.

Love changes your world.

Love changes your workplace.

Love changes your home.

Love changes your church.

Love changes your habits.

Love changes your leadership.

Love changes your everyday.

Love changes your thinking.

Love changes your heart.

Love changes your spirit.

Love changes your disciplines.

Love changes your language.

Love changes your listening.

Love changes your reading.

Love changes your pace.

Love changes your insufficiencies.

Love changes your hurts.

Love changes your reactions.

Love changes your temperament.

Love changes your generosity.

Love changes your gratitude.

Love changes your attitude.

Love changes your servanthood.

Love changes your ability to forgive.

Love changes your spiritual and emotional capacities.

Love changes how you use your gifting.

Love changes your compliments.

Love changes your discernment.

Love changes your tenacity.

Love changes your dreams.

Love changes your hustle.

Love changes you.

Love changes whatever it touches.

Love changes everything.

MARKED

It was my sixteenth birthday, and I had my sights set on a big present from my parents. I had been asking them for a new car. I had my license and all I needed was a vehicle that would start. I was not picky about what type of car, just anything that would get me out of the house more often than not.

I remember tearing through all the presents from my parents. There were definitely some interesting gifts in the mix: new socks, a Nintendo 64 game, a leather jacket. When I made it to the final wrapped gift, I was nervous that they had missed my request.

As I picked up the last bag, I thought this would be the moment. In this bag were the keys to my driving future. I mean, I could go get my own fast food. I could drive myself to school. I could drive my friends anywhere at anytime. Or I could just sit and jam to my NSYNC CD . . . the options were limitless! (And that last one is not true. Not true at all.)

Opening this final bag was the climactic moment of my six-teenth year. This is what dreams were made of. As I opened it, I pulled out a very old, very used Bible. What? I thought, "OK, maybe this is one of those cutout Bibles where you open the front cover and the keys are inside. My parents are so creative!"

But as I opened the Bible, I was disappointed to discover that it was indeed a real, brown leatherbound Bible that had to be from the 1970s or 80s.

Remember, I am a pastor's kid. I was raised in the church my entire life. I was on the front pew every Sunday for every service. I attended every revival meeting, every old ladies' prayer gathering, and any other form of service at my church. My mom hung Scripture verses all over our walls. (I'm not sure they worked, but I guess I turned out OK. So, moms, you may continue your Scripture wall decor.) I've been surrounded by Christianity in every format my entire life.

I remember thinking, "Really? Another Bible?" The first fifteen years of my life I had received at least one Bible a year. I had young men's Bibles, leadership Bibles—I even had a young women's Bible! I had every Bible imaginable, and now here was another one! I was confused and frustrated.

My dad could tell I disapproved of this gift and that my expectations for a beautiful vehicle were not met. He said to me, "Son, I know you wanted a car. But a Bible, that'll drive your life!" You may be clapping internally right now. I most assuredly was not. I could not believe this was actually happening!

Dad then told me to open the Bible and I would understand the significance of this gift. So I did. There were markings and highlights in the Bible, and it was taped together on the outside.

I realized it was the Bible he'd been preaching from. He told me he had preached from that Bible since the day I was born. That was a cool piece of information but not nearly enough to get me excited about it.

He then told me to open it to where he'd placed a bookmark. So I did, turning to the last page in the book of Micah. This was where they got my name. There on that page were the footprints of a baby. I looked at him again, wondering what I was seeing.

Dad explained those were my footprints. When I was born, he put my feet on an inkpad and then placed them on this page in the book I was named after. My demeanor began to change. He told me how he had saved this Bible for my sixteenth birthday. I never knew that my baby footprints were in his Bible until that moment.

When I received that Bible, I judged its value by what it looked like. It was beat up. It was held together by tape. Pages were missing. Clearly this book had been well used!

However, the moment I saw what was in it, it became priceless. How did something that you can buy from a bookstore at a reasonable price become priceless? How could this Bible become invaluable to me in a matter of seconds? How did I look past the blemishes to see this book's real worth?

I realized the value of this Bible did not come from its markings, its blemishes, or its missing pieces. Its value came from what it was marked with. It was marked with something irreplaceable. It was marked with something I could not produce myself. My dad picked me up as a baby and placed my feet on the Word. I was holding something no one else could give me.

I had judged that Bible because of what it looked like. It looked like it had been through some tough times. But it was the internal imprint that revealed its eternal value.

Love That Really Wins

The Bible says in 1 John 4:18 that perfect love casts out fear. When you accept perfect love, you are marked by that love. You are marked by a love that does not stay dormant in your life. In fact, this verse tells us how powerful real love is. Love will get to work once you allow it into your life. Real love will cast some things out of your life. Perfect love and fear cannot coexist. Have you allowed this perfect love to remove your fear or anxiety? Perfect love will work in you if you allow it. It will also work some things out of you if you allow it. Perfect love, which is Jesus, cannot coexist with sinful roommates.

The devil is not winning in your life; you're just allowing him in. How can a defeated foe claim victory over you? This is why the enemy does not want you to see how loved you are. The moment you embrace and accept perfect love, the devil goes back to his rightful position: under your feet. If you ever hear the devil talking to you again, I want you to tell him, "I don't speak loser." Because the truth is that when you realize the powerful love you've been marked with, you don't mess with a defeated devil. You now live victoriously in God's presence. You are not fighting for victory; you are fighting from victory. You no longer live for love but from love.

When Jesus died on the cross, he was nailed. Those nails left marks. Those marks indicate his love for you.

So look at yourself again. Not in the mirror. Not through the lens of failed dreams or broken aspirations. Look inside and see that you are marked. You are tattooed by the love of God. Nothing can separate you from God's love.

Why then do we feel separated and distant at times? It's not because his love isn't there but because we haven't acknowledged his love. God's love is ever present. Have you forgotten his promise to never leave or abandon you? Oftentimes seeing God's love requires a perspective change from us. Maybe the issue is that you are questioning God instead of challenging your perspective.

I've told this story about my footprints all over the world, and I have heard many reports of people now doing the same thing with their kids. I do it with mine, and I will give them their footprint Bibles when they are older. I pray it will teach them that value comes not from what you do but how you've been marked.

Tattooed Love

Hosea was a man marked by the love of God. Gomer, his wife, was a woman who never really found her mark. She was constantly looking externally for what can only be given internally. God's love works inside out. It changes your heart. It shifts your soul. It challenges your perspectives. It casts out your fears and worries.

It is vital to remember that Hosea represents Jesus and Gomer represents us. That may be hard to hear, but we are the sinners in this story. We are the ones who ran away from all that we needed and found ourselves in bondage.

Gomer was looking for something to complete her life. Was it another relationship? Satisfaction through temporary pleasures? And just like Gomer, we often run from the thing we need most. We wind up on the auction block, being sold to the highest bidder. We give ourselves away to whatever we deem most worthy or enticing. This is why people who have achieved financial success often struggle with depression or anxiety once they reach the goal they thought would bring them joy. Financial success is not a bad thing; it can totally be a good thing. But a good thing absent of the foundation of God becomes a poisonous thing. There is no true love or fulfillment outside of Jesus.

What is bidding for your soul? You'd better believe the devil is trying to take back your soul. The devil has a plan for you. That plan is to kill, steal, and destroy you. And if the devil can't destroy you, he will distract you.

I am reminded of Peter when he walked on the water to Jesus. Who knows what his intentions were? Was he trying to show off his faith in front of everyone, or was he genuinely trying to get to Jesus and do the miraculous? Peter was not destroyed by his experience; however, he became distracted when he saw the wind and waves. So possibly the most dangerous thing that can happen to us is not a day of destruction but a lifetime of distraction.

We live our lives in a rhythm of trying to find our mark, and breakdowns happen when we miss that mark. When you fail to fully acknowledge that God has marked you, you will allow things that have no value to define you.

We are on the auction block daily and the bids are flying. Our decisions reveal what we believe we've been marked by. When you see that you've been tattooed by the real love of God, you have no sell-out price. The world is not as attractive anymore. Social media doesn't bring the insecurity it once did. Opinions of others no longer discourage you. Instead, they empower you to be the best you.

My wife has a tattoo on her ankle that says "Beloved." What's even cooler about her tattoo is that the letters L-O-V-E-D are red while the rest of the letters are black, so it reveals another message: "Be loved."

You are God's beloved; now you must learn how to be loved. Just like a tattoo, you cannot remove God's love for you. Isaiah 49:16 even says that your name is tattooed on the palm of God's hand. His love has been inked on our hearts. It is time to live like you've been tattooed by a love you cannot erase.

Love That Purchases

Hosea bought back his wayward wife. It's interesting to note that Hosea's name means "salvation" and Gomer's name means "completion." Salvation showed up and found its completion once the price was paid. Hosea paid a price no one else was willing to pay. Jesus paid a price you and I could never pay. Salvation is complete when it finds a willing heart. A repentant heart. A heart open and ready to be marked by something real.

Hosea bought back his wife. He purchased what was already his. That's what Jesus did for us on the cross. What kind of love does it take to buy back the human race that you created? Yet God did. He paid to have us back in relationship with him.

It intrigues me to think that Salvation himself was walking around on dirty streets in a sinful world. God so loved us that he sent his Son. Jesus came to us, we didn't come to him. He went where he should have never gone: to dirty, sinful humanity. He could have saved us from a distance, but instead he chose relationship. He showed us the greatest example of life and then paid a price more expensive than we could ever pay. This is what the love of God did for us.

If you find yourself settling for fake "likes" and fake love, it's time to run to the One who knows you the best and find in him real love and validation. You were bought at a high price, so don't sell yourself short. Don't sell yourself for cheap thrills and one-night feels. Don't try to find love in all the wrong places.

You've been bruised. You've been hurt. Everyone has been. But not everyone has been healed. You will not find your healing in an opportunity or a relationship. You will not find your healing in your spouse. Marriage is beautiful when Jesus is the center, but that's just it: Jesus must be the foundation of all we do. And Jesus is the Great Physician. Jesus knows you better than you know yourself. Jesus's doors are always open to you. It is not about how greatly you've been hurt but how deeply you trust the love of God.

Decide right now to have a marriage marked by the love of God. Decide right now to have a dating life marked by this real love. Let me say this for any single people reading this book: don't date to find your value, date once you know your value. You're welcome.

Decide now to stop being marked by that offense you've carried for so long. Make up your mind to refuse the shame of failure you have been bound to because of negative words spoken over you. Decide in this moment to kick lust out the doors of your mind. Decide right now that you will no longer walk hand in hand with compromise. Decide right now to be defined by hope. Joy and peace will be the results you reap from a life planted in love.

You are not marked by that generational curse you cannot seem to kick. You are not marked by depression. You are not marked by suicidal thoughts. You are not marked by insecurities. You are not marked by the limitations you have placed on yourself. You are not marked by the mistakes of yesterday. You are not marked by the anxieties you constantly carry. You are not marked by the devil's lies over your life. Because none of those things paid the price for your life. They want to get your eyes off the one thing that will change everything, and that is the real love of Jesus.

You have been marked by the love of God. Because of this love, you have nothing to lose and nothing to prove. God's got you. You cannot scare away this love with sin. You cannot outrun this love if you tried. It is with you, for you, and always available to you.

Let this love be seen in your actions and in how you love others. Go the second mile for people, because that's what love would do. Help those in need. Step up and be the change for the sake of love. More than ever before, we need a love revival. However, we cannot give what we do not have. Once we accept this love in our lives, we must not be content for it to remain passive. This love is on a mission to change everything it can get ahold of.

Let love grip your existence. Let love flow out from you.

This is no fake kind of love.

This love changes everything.

NOTES

1. "Hosea: Introduction from the NIV Study Bible," The International Bible Society, https://www.biblica.com/resources/scholar-notes/niv-study-bible/intro-to-hosea/.

2. https://www.brainyquote.com/quotes/martin_luther_king_jr_297520.

3. "The Meaning of Numbers in the Bible: The Number 15," BibleStudy.org, http://www.biblestudy.org/bibleref/meaning-of-numbers-in-bible/15.html.

4. "The Meaning of Numbers in the Bible: The Number 5," BibleStudy.org, http://www.biblestudy.org/bibleref/meaning-of-numbers-in-bible/5.html.

5. C. S. Lewis, *Mere Christianity* (New York: Macmillan, 1943), 49.

6. Brennan Manning, *The Ragamuffin Gospel* (Colorado Springs: Multnomah, 1990), 90.

Micah Berteau is the lead pastor of The House Fort Worth, which he launched in February 2018 and is now one of the fastest-growing churches in America. His congregation already has thousands of members and has witnessed thousands of people coming to faith. The House has more than eleven thousand members between its campuses, including The House Modesto and The House Fort Worth. Micah is honored to travel and preach all over the world. His desire is to see everyone intimately know Jesus and to boldly make him known. He and his wife, Lindsey, have two sons and live in Fort Worth, Texas. Learn more at www.thehousefw.com.

Connect with
MICAH BERTEAU

WWW.MICAHBERTEAU.COM

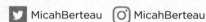 PastorMicahBerteau MicahBerteau MicahBerteau